Love Letters to My Garden

Barbara Blossom Ashmun

Illustrations by Linda Engstrom

Easy Chair Press
Portland, Oregon

Illustrator   Linda Engstrom
Editor   Brenda Jones
Designer   Tom Sumner

© 2017 Barbara Blossom Ashmun

ISBN: 978-0-9740392-1-3

Booktown
Production

Contents

Introduction	viii

Joy at Home — 2

The Garden, My Companion	3
Why I Garden	7
Calling All New Gardeners	11
Let's Have Some Fun	14
One Step at a Time	17
Island Beds Dress Up the Backyard	21
Sidetracked	26
The Sunbathers	29
Why My Garden Needs Cats	32
To Garden is Human, but to Sit, Divine	36

My People — 40

Finding My Mentors	41
Frank Teaches Me to Grow Tomatoes	44
Finding Faith	47
Herb Orange, the Great Liberator	50
Running After Ed Wood	55
Friends Live On in My Garden	58
When Your Inner Critic Scolds	62
Garden Fans from Afar, Unite!	65
We're All in This Together	68
Plant Snobbery Cured by a Visit Overseas	72
The Alligator Chain Saw Massacre	75
Just Say Yes: The Joys of an Open Garden	78

Plants — 82

- Why So Many Plants? — 83
- Torn Between Two Loves:
  - Plant Lust and Beautiful Design — 86
- Fiddling with Ferns — 90
- Making My Own Mistakes — 94
- Rocks and Roses — 98
- True Confessions of
  - a Garden Designer — 102
- A Love Letter to Shrubs — 106
- Plant Romance, Name or No Name — 110
- A Plant Collector's Secret — 114
- Plant Sale Tango — 118
- In Praise of Ordinary Plants — 122
- Agreeable Abelias — 126
- Can't Get Enough Conifers — 129

The Seasons — 134

- Winter Wonder — 135
- Winter Confessions — 137
- Let the Light Shine — 140
- Return of the Light — 143
- Just Play — 146
- Why We Love Spring the Most — 149
- Spring Surprises — 152
- Speedy is the Pace for Spring — 156
- Fleeting Beauty — 159
- The Best and the Worst
  - of Summer Color — 162
- Turning with the Seasons — 166
- Fall is the Time for Mellowing — 169
- Autumn Musings — 172

Accepting Change — 176

Creative Solutions:
- One Step at a Time — 177
- The Worried Gardener — 181
- Editing My Garden — 184
- Wishing for Something Else — 188
- Love the Garden You Have — 191
- In Praise of Small Pleasures and Ordinary Gardens — 195
- Kali Helps Me Garden — 198
- Go with the Flow — 201
- It's Hard to Let Go — 204
- From Despair to Hope When a Giant Tree Crashes — 207
- Transformation — 212

Acknowledgments — 216

In memory of my beloved

Aunt Libby,

who started it all.

Introduction

And then I realized what love did.
It changed your whole world.
—Alice Hoffman

NOT LONG AFTER I left New York for Portland, Oregon, in 1972, my favorite relative, Aunt Libby, died way too young. She was only in her early fifties, and when I hugged and kissed her goodbye in the hallway of her Manhattan apartment building that last Sunday evening we were together, she was crying because I was moving clear across the country. If I'd had any idea that I'd never see her again, I'd have been sobbing, too.

My father called one Sunday morning just a few months later with the sad news. "Your Aunt Libby passed away during gall bladder surgery—it was so unexpected," he said.

"On my God! How could this happen?" I could hardly breathe.

"Her heart couldn't take the stress," he said. A gray cloud hovered over my life. When my father shipped the antiques Aunt Libby had left me, I put my nose inside one of the copper pots to try to catch a whiff of her lemony perfume.

Shocked and bereft, I cried myself to sleep night after night. Terrified that I wouldn't remember what she looked like, I stared at her photograph, trying to memorize her face. Glowing black eyes, high cheekbones, a warm smile, curly black hair against porcelain white skin. In my childhood, Libby was always larger than life. A tall, zaftig woman, with a laugh that filled the room, she lit up our apartment with great joy when she came to visit. When she enveloped me in a hug, I knew I was loved.

Her gifts were always magical, imbued with love, and showed me how clearly she was aware of who I was. To the little girl who loved color, she gave a necklace of beads sparkling with all the colors of the rainbow. Later on she delighted me with a manicure set holding bottles of nail polish—pink, orange, red, silver, and gold. To the teenager, she gave a very grown-up genuine leather purse. And best of all, because she knew how much I hated the Yiddish name my parents gave me, with its harsh guttural sound, she gave me a nickname, Bromo-Seltzer, because I was "fizzy." Shortened to Bro, it became my new, happier name that my sister still uses.

Libby shaped my life with her loving presence, even after she was gone. In her will, she left me enough money for a down payment on my first home. The house came with a garden, and right next door lived Frank Curtis, an experienced gardener who took me under his wing and taught me everything I needed to know to get started.

And so began an adventure that altered my life. The garden taught me how to live fully, to be present to each moment, to be a witness to life unfolding. Each day brought a new miracle, from winter's earliest snowdrop to the last maple leaf on fire with autumn color. From a bookish, indoor social worker, I became an ardent gardener, living with the seasons and working outdoors in rain, in wind, and in sun, digging and raking, hauling and sawing, breathing in the fullness of life. I'd always loved beauty, and now a new kind of beauty was before me every day—a rainbow of flowers, sparkling droplets of rain at the edges of leaves, the sky turning lavender at the end of a long summer day.

More gifts came along with time: wonderful friends who share my obsession for gardening; a career as a garden designer, teacher and consultant; and a passionate need to write about what I love most. And so these love letters to the garden explore many aspects of my gardening life, especially the joy I find right here in my backyard, the plants themselves and their amazing qualities, the seasonal changes that come with the territory, the tribe of brother and sister gardeners who have helped and encouraged me, and the ongoing lessons that gardening has taught me, most of all learning to embrace change.

Joy at Home

The Garden, My Companion

*I worked out anguish in a garden. Without the
flowers . . . I might not have survived.*

—May Sarton

BACK IN THE 1960s, like most of my friends, I started smoking. There was something very comforting about pulling out a pack of cigarettes, lighting up, inhaling, and blowing out a long stream of smoke. Especially at a party, cigarettes and a Black Russian helped ease that tension preliminary to meeting strangers—with a drink in one hand and a cigarette in the other, all that maneuvering and puffing gave me something to do with my hands.

I can still remember the flick of the lighter or scratch of the match, followed by a flame in the dark and the hiss of smoldering paper as the cigarette burned down. I felt so sophisticated when my boyfriend lit two cigarettes at the same time and handed me one, just like Jean-Paul Belmondo in the movies. Cigarettes went with everything—talking on the phone, drinking coffee, leaving the office for home.

Of course the connection with lung cancer spoiled the romance of smoking. Still, even knowing all that and having quit for seven years, I started up again when I got divorced in 1977. I needed my little white friends to get through.

Fortunately, the second time around didn't last very long. I took up running after dumping that last pack of cigarettes in the garbage. And by then I had a much better friend—the garden. I couldn't have put it so clearly at that time, but I knew that no matter how blue or desperate I felt, if I just went out to the garden, pretty soon my dark mood would lift.

That summer of 1977, I rattled around in the beautiful 1925 four-bedroom house that was too familiar to leave, yet so strange to live in all alone. The dining table seemed so vast with only me sitting down to dinner. I started eating in the breakfast nook, a tiny alcove at the far end of the kitchen, where a small round table made me feel better. That was my cat Molly's favorite perch too—she'd look out on the bird bath in the garden and click her chops.

I turned my ex-husband Ray's upstairs office into a conservatory, filling it with plants. I found old benches at garage sales and painted them purple, and set clivias and scheffleras, gloxinias and African violets upon them. The big windows faced east, and everything flourished in that light.

But outdoors I felt much more comfortable. The garden had always belonged to me, so it felt like the same old friend as before and even more comforting during this tough time. It was the only place where the gnawing anxiety at the pit of my stomach would lift. It was as if every time I stuck a spade in the dirt, a little bit of fear spilled off the end of the blade and buried itself in the soil. Fear would drain away completely, as long as I kept gardening. Anger, too, found release when I dug, when I pruned, when I turned over the ever-growing compost pile behind the big laurel hedge.

Being alone in the garden felt so different from being alone in the house. Outdoors, there was no absence of Ray, and beyond that, the garden had a presence all its own. It flourished under my care and grew green and healthy with every bit of tending. Time took on a different feeling in the garden—I lost track of it. Time felt more spacious. One minute it was early afternoon and I had just begun, and the next minute the sky was turning orange with sunset. I drifted in and out of thoughts and feelings, starting out with heavy worries—how would I get through the upcoming weekend—and as I became more engrossed in digging out oxalis with my trowel, making sure to get every last bit of the root system, thoughts lost their shapes like clouds.

I decided that since my life had already turned upside down, I would make another big change. I would quit my job as a medical social worker, which I had never really liked, and see what else I could do. Strangely enough, without a partner, I felt freer to take chances and risk poverty. *If not now, when?* was my mantra. Janis Joplin's voice echoed through my mind:

> *Freedom's just another word*
> *for nothing left to lose.*

I didn't know what I would do next for a living; I just wanted more time to garden, to read, to see my friends, to write in my journal. Work was eating up my life. I promised myself a year of complete freedom and figured out how much I needed to save up to live for a year without working. It would take me three years to save that much, but once I made the decision to leave, a big weight lifted.

Meanwhile, gardening was such an inexpensive hobby, and so consoling, that I jumped in with abandon. I took advantage of working only ten minutes away from home to spend lunch hour in the garden. I got up early so I could at least see what was in bloom that morning before facing my job, where my small office had no windows. The cruel fluorescent lights had no warmth, and the sounds of doctors and nurses being paged overhead, phones ringing, and patients calling out for help were exhausting.

Each morning I stored up my garden's visual beauty and fragrance before passing through the doors of the hospital. The comfort of a warm breeze rippling though the rosemary stayed with me during the day. I pinned old calendar pages of irises and roses onto the walls of my office to bring the garden inside.

At home all I needed was a bucket to weed into, a few tools, and a hose with a watering wand on its end. Rock Creek Community College had bunny hutches in its agricultural area full of straw litter containing manure. Finding that the donut shop had great big white buckets they were happy to give away, I piled a few buckets into my sedan and drove out to the campus to clean out the hutches. In less than an hour, I had a trunk of manure-filled buckets to take back to the garden to mulch the beds and improve the soil.

This early appreciation for rabbit litter taught me the great value of recycling. In the early eighties I found a new friend who rescued domestic rabbits and was happy to give me as much rabbit litter as I could use to improve the soil in my second, much bigger garden. To this day I collect neighbors' leaves and coffee grounds from the neighborhood cafes. And the garden has remained a faithful companion, a place that gives me enduring comfort each day.

Why I Garden

Does this path have a heart? All paths are the same. They lead nowhere . . . Does this path have a heart is the only question. If it does, then the path is good. If it doesn't, it is of no use.
—Carlos Castaneda

THE OTHER DAY I came in from the garden and caught a glimpse of myself in the mirror. Who was that woman in the muddy jacket, hair sticking up like a punk rocker's, hands streaked with dirt, with a deliriously happy grin on her face?

What made me so euphoric on that particular September day? It was probably the scent of 'Summer Breeze' hummingbird mint, a blend of lemon, sugar, and mint wafting through the garden, so enticing that I ran my hands through the stems to release more and more aroma. Morning and evening, hummingbirds flocked to it, darting into the coral and pink tubular flowers for nectar.

It might have been the radiant pink flowers of the autumn crocus, blooming at the feet of hostas and epimediums, that lifted my spirits. Or the white flowers of autumn-flowering cyclamen gleaming in front of dark green hellebore foliage, or even the raindrops sparkling on the burgundy leaves of the purple smoke tree.

I garden to travel to the wonderland of sensory delights. Out there I'm a little kid digging in the dirt, abandoning all cares. I'm back in my wild childhood, before self-consciousness set in. Gardening sets me free.

Dressed in raggedy t-shirts and well-worn, stretched out pants that are soon splattered with mud, coated with compost, soil crumbs, seed pods, and grass clippings, I'm as much a part of the earth as a worm. A final layer of fuzzy fur comes courtesy of Blackjackie, the cat who strayed into my garden two years ago and decided to stay. She meows like a siren until I pet her, so to turn off her plaintive yowls, I weed with my right hand and pet her with my left. The instant I stop, she rubs up against my pants, shedding fine black hairs.

Blackjackie helps me slow down and notice what's happening in the garden. She jumps up on a garden bench and howls until I sit down beside her and stroke her coat, letting me know by head butts that she needs to have her head massaged continuously. As we sit there together, I look up to see that seven-son flower is dropping its white petals to expose the red calyxes. The tree is a study in white and red. Just minutes earlier I'd walked right by without paying any attention. I would have missed it entirely if it weren't for the cat.

One warm autumn afternoon Blackjackie hurled herself onto the lawn, tummy side up, to catch the sun. I thought she had a good idea, so I lay down beside her and stretched out, enjoying an upside-down view of the silver willow against a blue sky.

Every day the garden surprises me. After two days of drenching rain and winds so intense I was sure the young Chinese elm would snap off at the trunk, the tree still stands strong, green leaves shining in today's welcome sunlight. The six-foot tall castor bean plants went from vertical to horizontal, and as I trimmed the gorgeous red leaves to free the plants beneath them, I saved plenty of seed pods for next year's crop.

It was close to dusk when I was watering the pots and a flicker of yellow caught my eye. There on the rim of the purple birdbath stood a tiny yellow bird. Hopping along, it circled the rim. Did it want a drink? A bath? Finally it bobbed its small head down to the water and took a dainty sip. Then it scurried some more and bobbed again, dipping delicately into the water for another small sip. This went on repeatedly as I stood there spellbound, holding the hose and overwatering the pots.

My garden is a blend of today, yesterday and tomorrow, of this season, past seasons, and future ones. Stout grape vines planted fifty years ago by old Mr. Berg, who lived here first, continue to bear, along with apple trees whose gnarled trunks are reminders of the stalwart beauty of old age. The 'Desert King' fig tree began as a cutting which I rooted in damp sawdust, and the thirty-foot silver willow once grew in a gallon pot at Heronswood Nursery.

But beyond the pleasures of color and scent, of flowers and fruit, there's the great joy of tending, of caring for, of working with the soil, water, air, and sun to grow life. Like the plants, I need to feel the sun and rain on my face, the wind in my hair, the soil running through my fingers. I need to breathe in the fresh air and be out there as the seasons turn, no matter how cold or hot.

When I give myself to the garden—digging, raking, planting, mulching, pruning—all sense of linear time falls away. Worry and fear blow away on the breeze and I'm left with a sense of ease and wonder. More and more lately, I stand before the vivid 'Heart Throb' dahlias, before the purple 'Enor' penstemons, and whisper, "You are so beautiful!"

In the garden, the line between work and play vanishes. When I'm moving the big pile of wood chips from the shoulder of the road to the paths and passersby urge me not to work so hard, I just smile—only similarly smitten gardeners understand how much fun I'm having. If I were to give my garden a name, it would be Barbara's Playground.

Many years ago, long before I became a gardener, I

drove along a meandering country road in Maine, right around that magical time when the sun is low in the late afternoon sky and the fields are bathed in golden light. I was struck by a scene that sank deeply into my consciousness. An old woman in faded clothing knelt in her garden, weeding. She looked so serene, so engrossed in her work that she never even once looked up at my car.

That would be the life, I thought to myself. And that small thought remained lodged somewhere inside me for a very long time, dormant as a nasturtium seed in winter. I am that woman now, and the garden is my true home, much more so than the rooms inside my house.

Calling All New Gardeners

*Beauty happens unexpectedly, but it comes out
of a practice of attention and humility. And beauty
is always a surprise. You can't go expecting beauty. It
comes from tilling those fields . . . It takes
imagination to catalyze it . . .*

—Tom Jay

IF YOU HAVEN'T ALREADY gardened and experienced the pleasure of growing your own flowers and vegetables, it's never too late. Some gardeners are lucky enough to grow up beside a green-thumbed grandmother or have a neighbor who initiates them into the mysteries of seed and soil, but anyone can dive in at any time. A little patch of earth, a few seeds, some water, and you're at the starting line.

You don't need a fancy wardrobe. Most of us live in well-worn jeans, sweatshirts, and waterproof boots. But it does help to cultivate a few qualities that you can't buy anywhere, not even online.

First, a sense of friendly curiosity. Curiosity about plants and how to nurture them, whether luscious tomatoes that grow from the tiniest seeds or velvety roses that spring from thorny sticks. Curiosity about a wildly contorted tree in a neighbor's garden that you ask about and discover is a Camperdown elm. Curiosity about colors and how they enhance each other to make a painterly garden—how orange and pink create iridescence, how purple and yellow make each other pop, how red gives vitality to the picture. Curiosity about the varieties of scent, from sweet mock orange to pungent eucalyptus to downright stinky voodoo lilies. A sense of discovery about the soil and its inhabitants, from earthworms to beetles; about visitors like chickadees and hummingbirds; about nurseries to visit and places to travel where great gardens wait to be explored.

A fertile imagination will help you make the garden of your dreams. Imagination blooms early in the morning, late at night, and whenever there is enough quiet to hear its soft voice and notice its visions. A sweep of pastel peonies, or dazzling dahlias, or lacy ferns embroidering a woodland floor may appear in your imagination just as you are waking up one morning. You may remember the perfume of lilacs in your auntie's garden, or a sunny meadow from your childhood where you lay on the grass, watching the clouds stream by. Images that speak to your heart will appear to guide you on your way.

You'll need determination to keep on gardening in the face of windstorms that blow down trees and extreme cold that kills tender hebes. You'll need persistence to combat sucking aphids, voracious slugs, and cruel cutworms. You'll need dedication to protect plants to the best of your ability, to look death in the face when it comes, and then drive to the nursery for replacements.

Without a good sense of humor, you're lost. The whole business of gardening is a big joke if you think about it for a minute. You'll start with soil that's imbalanced—too much clay, too much sand, or too many rocks—and spend years amending it with manure, compost, bone meal, lime, blood meal, and oyster shells. You'll spend more money on manure than on groceries! It will be hard not to laugh when you catch a glimpse of yourself in the mirror, bundled up in fleece, wearing surgical gloves, rubber boots, and old jeans splattered with mud. Not to mention a mad bomber hat lined with fake fur to combat the biting cold.

You've got to have guts to grow what you love. Never mind what the neighbors think—if you want to tear out the lawn and grow blueberries, summon up your courage and go for it.

Years ago, a friend brought her husband by my garden in winter to show him the cottage garden style she wanted for her own place. "What a mess!" he said, looking at the dormant front yard with nothing but the bare branches of mock orange and roses, with the slimy old leaves of daylilies and Siberian irises. He couldn't picture the explosion of radiant flowers that my friend remembered from past summers. My winter garden was sparse, with only red twig dogwoods and a few evergreens to console me. But back then, I lived for spring, summer, and fall when I was out in Flowerland all day long. Grow the garden of *your* dreams; make *yourself* happy.

Let desire call out to you and have its way. Even the most experienced gardeners crave at least another dozen lilies, a few more clematis, or just one more beautiful container, birdbath, or a better hose—this time one that really doesn't kink. Desire is what keeps us going, feeds our passion, and propels us towards next spring when we will make the garden ever so much better. Don't hesitate, even if you've never tried it—the garden is calling out for you to jump in.

Let's Have Some Fun

Gardening, like living, should be fun.
—Christopher Lloyd

RECENTLY I TOOK A WORKSHOP on writing thrillers. The one piece of advice that I remember was actually a question the instructor asked. "Are you having fun? If you're not enjoying it, don't do it."

I thought a lot about how many situations that applies to. Friendships. Work. Gardening! If we're not having fun, it's time to reconsider how we'd rather spend our time.

It's easy to turn gardening into a series of chores and call it "yard work." Sounds like prison, doesn't it? Recently on a day when I was getting sidetracked, picking off dandelion flowers and weeding instead of planting, I heard a little voice in my head complaining, *I'm not getting anywhere!* I had to laugh—where was there to go? I was having fun, doing whatever was calling to me!

When I remember that the garden is mine to enjoy, mine to fall in love with, mine to putter in or to work to exhaustion, I have a blast. The unexpected surprises make gardening the most fun for me. Digging down into the damp soil under the apple tree where apples and leaves have composted for years I come upon big fat earthworms wriggling around, their shiny pink bodies full of life. They tell me the soil is alive and well. So much is going on underground! While I weed around the rosemary, inhaling the minty smell, a hummingbird rockets by my head for a taste of fuchsia nectar, its red iridescent head sparkling in the sunlight.

On an especially wet day I look out the window and see two mallard ducks swimming in the little bog, bobbing up and down for their breakfast. Peering through binoculars, I revel in their beauty. His glossy green head, yellow beak, and white neck ring are showier than her chocolate feathers with only a dash of cobalt blue, and both waddle off on bright orange feet.

When the rain gets to be just too much, I head for the garden center and stock up on big bags of planting compost to enrich the soil in a bed I'm renovating, as well as bagged potting soil for the containers. I consider various trellises and arbors, daydreaming about whether they might look good in the garden. I'll have to take a better look at possible places for them before I commit.

One morning there's a knock on the door, and it's a tree service with free wood chips for my paths. Yes! They unload the truck onto the shoulder of my front yard, leaving a mound as big as a car. I'm thrilled to have these wood chips smelling of spruce to move onto the paths. Another excuse to avoid the gym—I'll get plenty of aerobic exercise wheelbarrowing those loads to the backyard. Not just great for topping paths, these wood chips make good mulch around hydrangeas and hardy fuchsias, holding in moisture and discouraging weeds from germinating.

I anxiously watch for the first signs of life on hardy fuchsias growing in big containers at the edges of a bed. At last, small green shoots appear at the base of the woody stems. They're alive! Similarly, it's a relief to see the first hosta noses poking out of the ground, pushing through the damp soil for another season. The clumps are wider than last year, promising a bigger, more flamboyant show of golden and blue-green leaves. It's time to get out the slug bait to protect the newly emerging foliage from chew holes.

I notice the 'King' apple tree is blooming once more, despite the cavity in one of the big limbs. Some seven years ago, a friend who was pruning the tree warned me that the tree was going downhill, and I expected it to decline immediately. But no, it continues to produce plentiful apples, maybe the same way we learn to make the most of life, even in the face of weaknesses and limitations. "Lead with your strength" is a mantra I picked up from *What Happy People Know,* a favorite book. I think the apple tree has mastered this lesson.

Another pleasure is watching the first dahlia shoots emerge in their containers in the greenhouse. I always worry that they may have rotted or frozen over the winter—I don't keep the greenhouse very warm, and the pots look totally barren until the first green shoots sprout. In summer when those yellow, pink, and coral dahlias bloom, the effort of hauling those heavy pots in and out of the greenhouse pays off.

This time of year, I love to watch fern croziers do their dance, rising up from the bundle of knots at their center. Unfurling each day just a little more, the fronds spread their wide, lacy, green wings. As the ferns expand, the earlier-blooming daffodils decline, flowers and leaves turning dull and papery. In the garden, everything is in motion, flowers arriving and departing, life flowing in a stream of constant change.

A big part of enjoying my garden is making up my own mind about what I like. Maybe pink and yellow are just fine together, in spite of what the experts say. If I want to plant just one of every kind of perennial and enjoy a mishmash instead of an organized mass effect, that's my business. Then again, if I change my mind and edge entire bed with 'Obsidian' coral bells or orange geums, so be it. It's my garden, and I'm gonna have fun!

One Step at a Time

> *If we persist, I do not doubt that by age 96 or so we will all have gardens we are pleased with, more or less . . . And in plugging right along, patience, and freedom from fretting, are supreme gardening virtues.*
>
> —Henry Mitchell

MY GARDEN IS TURNING 30 this year! When I look out the window at the long vista, I'm filled with amazement and gratitude. This haven, a quiet retreat that I enjoy every day with song sparrows and flickers for company, has grown very slowly into a park-like setting.

I can easily remember what it was like back in 1986. Excitement and fear washed over me in equal doses as I looked around an acre of mostly waist-high field grass with a few fruit trees dotted here and there. I felt both thrilled and overwhelmed by the property's sheer size. Where would I begin?

I'd just left a city garden overflowing with flowers. Moving furniture, clothing, and books was a breeze compared to transplanting my garden. A parade of pickup trucks, vans and station wagons, driven by kind friends, hauled flats of hellebores, peonies, daylilies, irises, bellflowers, delphiniums, sedums, and Michaelmas daisies. A young 'Desert King' fig tree that continues to bear countless figs every summer, a Japanese aralia, and several hydrangeas made the trip. I wish I could have taken the wonderful well-amended soil with me, but I did carry buckets of compost from the long pile I'd built for many years behind the old laurel hedge. Dozens of daffodils and tulips came along, together with pesty hitchhiker seeds of

Labrador violets, feverfew and forget-me-nots, hiding in the soil around the bulbs.

All these plants patiently waited in tubs, buckets, and flats while I walked back and forth at the new property, trying to figure out where to start. Back then, I designed gardens as part of my living. For clients, I drafted a plan to scale on a blueprint. But designing on paper was never the way I'd made my own garden.

For me, two streams of activities flowed side by side. First I collected vast numbers of plants that called to me from the benches of nurseries and garden centers. Each had some unique feature that grabbed me. It might be a luscious color like the iridescent orange flowers of 'Westerland' rose. Or a compelling texture like the velvety petals of 'Karma Choc' dahlia, or the lacy leaves of 'Imperialis' cutleaf alder. Sometimes it was a riveting shape that caught my eye, say the layered look of the doublefile viburnum or the zigzagging branches of 'Unryu' camellia. I'm a pushover for scent too—I adore the piercing sweetness of Hall's honeysuckle and the sweet perfume of rugosa roses, especially 'Hansa'.

Then, with plenty of plants on hand, I'd stare at the garden's blank canvas and daydream about endless possibilities until I could see a painting coming to life.

This is my intuitive way of gardening. Driven by plant lust, I fall in love with particular plants. Later on, I figure out where to put them and how to combine them with each other. I have to stock up on lots of colors before I pick up my paintbrush. Plenty of plants from my first garden got me started on the next one, and a relentless passion to collect more varieties kept the garden evolving over time.

Although this process might sound a bit mysterious, some practical needs helped me decide what to do first. For example, my one-story house faced a road carrying bright yellow buses to the nearby school, so screening the road with tall plants was urgent.

I decided to remove the large front lawn and replace it with a mixed border. Woody shrubs would run down the middle like a backbone, with masses of perennials flanking them on both sides, one swathe facing the house and another facing the road. That was the overall concept. The specific plants have changed over the years as I learned from experience.

Deaths by drowning—a magnolia, several daphnes, and a gas plant succumbed—taught me to become more savvy about what thrives in sopping soil. I read, visited gardens and took horticulture classes to find out which plants could survive wet winters and dry summers.

Now red twig and yellow twig dogwood shrubs, a dwarf lilac, a silver willow, and *Rosa glauca* form the woody backbone creating privacy from the road. Step by step, over time, I changed out the plants to suit the current conditions. While it was still sunny, Siberian irises, daylilies and peonies were mainstays, but as the shrubs and trees grew taller and the bed became shadier, I replaced the irises and peonies with hostas, epimediums and ferns.

Unlike the smaller, more manageable front yard, some fifty feet from the road, the backyard stretched two hundred feet long. How would I approach this vast expanse without getting overwhelmed?

When I'd been a social worker, I learned about "partializing"—dividing a big problem into smaller pieces. I decided to divide the daunting backyard into a smaller upper section that I'd tackle first, and a lower longer portion that I'd think about later. To make this happen, I needed a wall to visually separate the two areas. If I'd had all the money in the world I'd have built a lovely brick wall with an arched gate, but on a limited budget I put my plants to work. A long narrow compost pile that remained from the former owner already stood around fifty feet from the back of the house, and there I planted all of the old-fashioned Michaelmas daisies from my old garden. Nourished by the rich compost, they took off in a rush of enthusiasm, quickly grew six feet tall, and hid the lower backyard.

I added other tough and fast-growing perennials from my stash to thicken this long border—spiderwort, feverfew, bellflowers and Santa Barbara daisy. Eventually I replaced them all with more interesting shrubs and perennials, but to begin with, they were just what I needed. The lower backyard was out of sight and out of mind! Now I could concentrate on the space closer to the house.

Looking back on my younger self, so full of excitement and with so little experience, I can see clearly that gardening is an act of courage. We must be brave to dive in with just a little knowledge and learn over time, polishing and refining as we grow along with the garden. Passion drives us forward, along with helpful friends who are ahead of us on the path. And what a sweet, sweet journey it is!

Island Beds Dress Up the Backyard

> *The insatiable plantsman soon discovers there are more plants than places to put them, and . . . there's no choice but to make an island bed. If this process continues, the garden eventually becomes islands of plants with grass paths between them.*
>
> —Pamela Harper

SO THERE I STOOD in the upper backyard, now screened from the lower portion by the helpful Michaelmas daisy hedge. The worst eyesore was a big bald patch with a wooden post bearing an electrical outlet smack in the center. Neighbors explained that an old RV had been parked there for years. What could I possibly do with that mess?

A couple of ideas fell into place like pieces of a jigsaw puzzle. I wanted to reduce the lawn, and here was a grass-free area just waiting to be planted. On a recent tour of English gardens, I'd visited Alan Bloom's Bressingham Gardens in England. He was the King of Perennials, showcasing them in more than forty island beds packed with dazzling color. Neon orange pokers, blue bellflowers, and purple penstemons bloomed riotously with a backdrop of weeping willows and pink flowering dogwoods. Nearby an ancient stone hut and a bridge, surely with trolls waiting beneath, were straight out of *Grimms' Fairy Tales*.

Bloom was like no gardener I'd ever seen before. A tall man with long white hair, bushy eyebrows, two gold hoop earrings, and a fierce look in his eyes, he reminded me of an elderly pirate. I'd first heard him speak in Seattle at a Hardy Plant study weekend and even though I didn't understand a single word of his British Latin, his slides were enough to win me over completely. So walking around his garden in England was a huge thrill. If only I could have island beds like his!

Back home from the tour, contemplating that barren ugly space, I thought, *Why not turn this into the first of several island beds?* Yes! I was no pirate, but I could imitate Bloom's style; after all there aren't any copyrights on garden design. I removed more grass and shaped the irregular bald patch into a generous circle. I prefer curves to straight lines, so this step launched a garden signature: rounded islands overflowing with perennials. Each year, I carved out at least one more island, erasing more and more lawn.

At first, I was so in love with perennials, I didn't mind the work. Staking, deadheading, dividing, fertilizing, watering—I did whatever it took. I stuffed that first island with delphiniums, speedwells, lilies, moss campions, cottage pinks, cranesbills, penstemons, and lamb's ears.

Color was enough at the beginning, but over time, I realized something was missing. As I walked around the perimeter, every plant was visible, with no place for faded flowers or tattered leaves to hide. Not only that, but the cottage pinks and cranesbills at the edge of the island fell face forward onto the lawn, and every time the lawn was mown these flowers had their heads chopped off. My first trick was to shove a big rock underneath these drapers so that they lounged against the hard surface, but that quick fix wasn't enough.

Frustrated at the sloppy look of my first island, I tried some experiments to see if I could improve things. I needed some edging plants to hold in the billowing perennials and also to keep out the lawn grass that kept sneaking into the bed. In England, gardeners often planted dwarf boxwoods for that purpose, but they were too formal for my blowsy garden. English writer Margery Fish recommended boxleaf honeysuckle as a good edger, and I planted a few and kept them trimmed, but after a few years they ran underground and formed colonies way too big for island beds, so out they came.

What if I found some perennials with good leaves to frame the island bed? They would have to be evergreen to hold the picture year round, or look good for at least three seasons. I thumbed through garden books, paid attention in gardens I visited, and eventually came up with a handful of reliable plants that were tall enough to keep the lawn out and also hug the perennials within. With a strong enough frame, the island would stand like a finished painting instead of a smudged one that blurred into the lawn.

By this time, years had gone by and four island beds were in various stages of development, still open to polishing and refining. Thanks to genius hybridizers, more and more new varieties of coral bells, avens, epimedium, and hellebores had sprung up. These plants would make reasonably easy-care edgers.

The lobed and sometimes ruffled leaves of coral bells now came in a wide assortment of colors, with some happiest in sun and others best in shade. 'Obsidian', 'Dolce Licorice', 'Mahogany', and 'Midnight Rose' would frame the sunny island beds, while 'Lime Marmalade', 'Green Spice', 'Sashay', and 'Frosted Violet' would edge the shadier ones.

Similarly, numerous avens with attractive leaves and long-blooming yellow and orange flowers were now on the market. Some, like 'Fireball' and 'Totally Tangerine', were gorgeous but bulky, more suitable towards the middle of an island where their masses of flower spikes could be supported by low edging frames. Shorter ones like 'Cooky', 'Mai Tai', 'Fire Storm', 'Eos', and 'Tequilla Sunrise' worked well at the front line.

As seasons have rolled into years, I have continued to delight in discovering new favorites for my island beds.

A little harder to find but worth the search, red-flowering 'Monarch's Velvet' potentilla also has shapely leaves and a long bloom period. For shade, epimedium rocks, with heart-shaped leaves that look good year round and sprays of early spring flowers in shades of yellow, red, pink, lavender, and even white. Again, kudos to the brilliant hybridizers who came up with some of my favorite varieties of this plant for edging beds, like 'Sweetheart', 'Frohnleiten', 'Kaguyahime', and 'Cherry Tart'. An older evergreen variety that's completely reliable and spreads vigorously, 'Sulphureum' is especially useful in dry shade where it lights up the garden with yellow flowers.

Hellebores also get highest marks for their dark green evergreen leaves and flowers lasting all the way from January through early spring—pink, yellow, white, green, burgundy, even speckled. I love them all. They've been such prolific self-sowers that I've given away hundreds of extras.

Over the years I've discovered that it helps to anchor island beds by adding some sculptural elements—otherwise they seem to float in the lawn. I like to place a metal sculpture, a ceramic birdbath, or a large ceramic container somewhere off-center. If the island is big enough, I'll place several pots within it. Planting dahlias in these large containers is also a way of adding brilliant summer color.

Especially when part of an island is shaded, I've learned to pay attention to the amount of light. Two of my islands are half in full sun and half in afternoon shade. On the sunny sides I concentrate on daylilies, sedums, and low-growing ornamental grasses. Where it's shadier, I continue the flow of daylilies (they can take half shade) for unity, and add shade-loving hostas, ferns, and saxifrages.

If I were starting over again, I'd raise all the island beds up a couple of feet, add compost for fertility and crushed rock for drainage, and surround them with low rock walls. Then I'd arrange to be born in England, into Alan Bloom's family. Just imagine, I would be Barbara Blossom Bloom!

Sidetracked

*Now in spring gardeners are irresistibly drawn to their gardens
... they are on the beds, presenting their rump to the splendid
azure sky; here they crumble a warm clod
between their fingers, there they pull out a weed ...*
—Karel Capek

AFTER WEEKS OF RAIN and 40-degree days, at last the sun appeared and the spring air warmed up so much I could just about watch the green spears of Solomon's seal growing taller by the minute.

On that first mild April day I set out to feed the plants. I plopped a 50-pound bag of slow-release organic fertilizer in the wheelbarrow, along with an old yogurt container as a scoop. I figured it would take about an hour to get around the entire acre and sprinkle each bed.

But I only got ten feet from the door when I noticed that a 'Gold Ring' barberry and a red twig dogwood were both reaching out long branches and strangling the poor Meyer lilac. I ran to the garage for my loppers and started pruning the two interlopers. As beautiful as purple-leaved barberries are, they're also wickedly thorny.

Wedged between the lilac, the dogwood, and the barberry, I bent to prune but rebounded each time the barberry stabbed me. I hoped no neighbors were watching my jittery dance. Soon the lawn was littered with branches, the lilac was free, and all three bushes shared the space democratically, at least for the time being.

Back to fertilizing, I sprinkled the north bed where Mexican orange was newly budded. White flowers were getting ready to bloom and waft fragrance into the garden. 'Constance' clematis buds were colored up pink and might open as soon as next week. In its third year, the clematis was finally scrambling up the Mexican orange and into the purple smoke tree.

But below the shrubs I noticed sad-looking ferns, still hanging on to last year's frayed leaves. Surely their new fronds were just about ready to unfurl from cozily curled-up croziers hiding beneath the older leaves like furry fists. I stooped down and carefully snipped away the old leaves, stopping to admire the nested croziers, still at rest. I pictured them slowly uncurling like party favors. Returning to the wheelbarrow, I filled the container again and continued to sprinkle fertilizer.

While I sprinkled, I saw bright green leaves bursting forth along the hydrangea branches, and below them epimedium was blooming with sprays of flowers like baby columbines—yellow, pink, lavender, white, even orange. Blue anemones carpeted the garden floor along with way too many Labrador violets, their leaves and flowers both purple. I really do love the way they spring up here and there with their cheerful faces, even if they are too much of a good thing.

I made my way to the backyard and took a breath, gazing at the big stretch of garden before me: the round island beds, the grape arbor, the greenhouse that looks like a spaceship, and the old 'Elephant Heart' plum tree filled with a haze of white flowers. Drifts of buttery yellow daffodils shone in the sun, while stretches of wine, pink and white hellebores lit up the shady beds. These hellebores, many grown from seed, have been multiplying for nearly thirty years and have naturalized into friendly colonies. But oh, no! Cresses and dandelions had sprouted between them, practically overnight. I pulled my trowel from its holster on my belt and started weeding. Bright green English laurel seedlings had also poked up through the damp soil, and I yanked them out as well.

By now there was more than a quick handful of weeds, so I ran to the potting shed and grabbed a bucket for the debris. The fertilizer sat in the wheelbarrow, waiting. Half an hour later, I got back to sprinkling. Soon I noticed creamy yellow flowers adorning branches of winter hazel and below, white and blue lungworts with bursts of deeper blue grape hyacinth. Spring's first new bronze leaves were emerging all along the Katsura tree branches, arranged in small symmetrical pairs of hearts, so beautiful and fresh.

I was really making progress now. About halfway down the backyard, I felt that great sense of accomplishment that comes with nearly getting the job done. That was when I saw the Persian ironwood tree, newly leafed out with this year's pleated, beech-like leaves. But marring its beauty were branches crossing each other in a wild tangle. I couldn't bear it, so I ran back to the garage for the long-handled loppers. I removed several branches growing toward the center of the tree and trimmed a few distracting side shoots. After a number of judicious cuts, the tree stretched out its limbs clearly and gracefully. But then, out of the corner of my eye I saw a huge butterfly bush reaching to the sky. It should have been pruned by now, but somehow I'd missed it. With a sudden surge of adrenaline I whacked that shrub way back to two feet from the ground. Now the path was littered with branches, and some day this week I would chop them up and haul them to the yard debris can.

By now the sun had disappeared behind the tall Doug firs in the distance. I parked the wheelbarrow with the bag of fertilizer right where I'd left off, like a bookmark. Tomorrow was another day, when I might just finish the job.

The Sunbathers

You have to keep them, Barbara.
They're part of the landscape now.
—Katy McFadden

THE SUNBATHERS ARRIVED in segments—legs, arms, torsos, and heads of two nude female figures made of high-fired terra-cotta. Sculptor Katy McFadden wheeled them into the garden on a hand truck and asked me where I wanted them. I felt a stab of fear in the pit of my stomach. These girls were so big, larger than life-size, and their heads had no hair—I just couldn't picture where on earth they could sit without dominating my garden.

At that time, more than twenty years ago, I didn't know much about placing garden sculpture and never pictured having any in my own garden. But Katy was eager to display her work in an outdoor setting, and offered to set them up and even host an art show in my garden. I'd agreed to the idea, but now that I saw the actual sculptures, I wasn't so sure. The Sunbathers were huge, stark naked, and bald!

"Let's try them under the grape arbor," I said in a faint voice. At least in that large space, off to the side, they wouldn't be overwhelming. There in the shade of the grapes they could rest less conspicuously than out in the open. Maybe they'd even be hidden if we placed them deep inside the bed.

But they didn't really look right there. After all they were sunbathers, and they begged to be out in a meadow. The two reclining figures were made to lean against each other, totally relaxed, as if they were basking in a sunny field on a warm summer day.

After a month of adjusting to their sheer size, I found

the courage to move them to the edge of an open, sunny border at the lower end of the garden, where they became a bold focal point. The garden was fairly new at that time and I planted masses of annuals to fill in around them, then added some perennials for the long run.

The early photographs of The Sunbathers show them lounging in a meadow of red, pink, and orange zinnias and dahlias. A tall gray cardoon with big jagged leaves accompanies them off to one side. They became a magnet for the lower garden—visitors, especially non-gardeners, were drawn there to gaze at the two nude women.

"It's Adam and Eve!" said a neighbor girl.

"Look again—they're actually Eve and Eve," I said, laughing.

"They need hair, and some clothing!" said my twin neighbor boys. One boy turned two pulp paper pots upside down, and plopped them on The Sunbathers' heads for hats, and the other threw a whole bunch of grass clippings on their bare breasts. This was getting kinda crazy!

After a few years the perennials grew up. Tall stands of Joe Pye weed with mauve flower domes, stretches of purple coneflowers, and the pale yellow flowers of 'Moonbeam' tickseed surrounded The Sunbathers. They began to look more natural, part of the landscape, as flowers tickled their backs and bloomed at their feet. Lady's mantle and forget-me-not seeds blew into the bed, and soon The Sunbathers were soaking in a froth of blue forget-me-nots each spring and bathing in waves of chartreuse lady's mantle in summer. Their feet and calves disappeared in the foam of flowers. They looked like they were taking a bubble bath.

Sadly, the coneflowers vanished along with the Joe Pye weed and the tickseed. It was just too soggy in this low-lying bed. I planted an assortment of red twig dogwoods, with green, gold and variegated leaves, and they grew happily behind The Sunbathers. Hot pink cranesbills seeded down into the bed, by bird or by wind, along with catchflies sporting clouds of pink flowers. The plant palette has changed, but The Sunbathers will remain lounging forever, steady and calm. They've become the signature of my garden. Whenever my garden is photographed for magazines or books, The Sunbathers are the center of attention.

In 2006 I was asked to pose for Soul of the Soil, a calendar to benefit a garden for children. I said yes right away—it was for a good cause. And then came the catch: those of us who agreed to this would have to pose nearly naked, like the famous calendar girls.

Even though I offered to stand behind a tree like that famous photograph of Imogene Cunningham by Judy Dater, or in the midst of some ornamental grasses, the photographer insisted that I recline alongside The Sunbathers. It was a chilly autumn day, and I joined the pair on the ground. Although my cats George and Ringo often stretched out on their toasty terra-cotta chests in summer's warmth, this was my first time to keep company with The Sunbathers. I hid behind their massive bodies, and held on to one of their shoulders as I reclined, peeking out between a torso and a knee. I actually felt petite behind these Amazons. I was wearing a wedding veil to celebrate the publication of my sixth book, *Married to My Garden*, not nearly as daring as the unapologetically naked sunbathers.

Perhaps some warm summer night I'll sneak out into the garden and hang out with the girls again. Every autumn they make a bold picture with masses of red twig dogwoods and a curtain of giant maiden grass behind them. I can see them in every season from my office window, stalwart figures in the ever-changing garden.

Why My Garden Needs Cats

Now I walk in beauty, beauty is before me,
beauty is behind me, above and below me.

—Navajo Prayer Song

IT'S EASY FOR ME to get too serious about gardening, worrying about having the most perfect garden and cutting-edge plants. Cats are the perfect cure for fretting and obsessing; they know how to luxuriate in the garden without doing a stitch of work. They know how to look beautiful without any effort.

Two orange tabbies were mine for sixteen years. Chunky George, the color of a camel, and bouncy Ringo, brighter orange with white stripes—along with visiting cats of all colors from the neighborhood—showed me how to just hang out.

There was charcoal-gray Jack, a tough troublemaker from down the block who hissed and spat at my two beloved tabbies but refused to go home. I'd chase him to the front yard and even down the driveway, but no, he insisted on staying. He'd plant himself under a big red twig dogwood where I couldn't reach him with the hose and take his afternoon nap in the shade.

You'd think an acre would be big enough for an entire tribe of cats, but occasionally fights erupted that had to be broken up with quick jet of water from the hose. Still, most of the time, numerous cats prowled the paths and borders, and were found sunning themselves on the warm brick patio or snuggled up between ornamental grasses, taking a well-deserved nap.

For cats are big believers in relaxation. Artist Wendy

Dunder's greeting card with a cat sprawled out on the front says it well: "The gospel according to cats: idleness wastes time; repose luxuriates in it." Cats in your garden will show you the many ways to rest without guilt.

A favorite place to relax is the top of the picnic table where a cat can practice yoga and stretch to its full size, especially in the downward dog pose that should really be called "downward cat." Ringo loved to lounge on this ample table, for he had such long legs that when he was a kitten, he looked more like a small pony. He was the official garden greeter who trotted down the driveway and meowed a welcome to every guest, waving his tail up in the air like a furry banner. Ringo's role as a host took a lot of energy and required a lot of rest, especially before open gardens when hundreds of visitors must personally be greeted and escorted to the backyard.

From the beginning Ringo was a big singer, meowing and yowling with all his heart and purring with a motor so strong it would put a snoring man to shame. Caruso seemed a suitable name for such a loud performer, but it was too serious—Ringo was just right for such a lively cat who was really a more casual, sixties kind of guy.

George, my husky orange tabby, favored warm spots, preferably between large clay pots where he could toast himself with stored heat. He loved The Sunbathers, Katy McFadden's larger-than-life ceramic sculptures. The same caramel color as their terra-cotta bodies, George blended right in until you got close and realized there was a cat nestled into their cleavage.

Gray and white Kit Kat actually lived next door but spent most summer days lounging on the benches under the grape arbor or resting up in an Adirondack chair between hunting sprees. It was Kit Kat who left me rodent trophies, for I would find them the morning after her midnight adventures when my own two tabbies were indoors merely dreaming of mice.

Then there was Blackjackie, an adorable tuxedo who showed up in the garden as a kitten. I figured she was my neighbor's kitty, but no one on my block or on craigslist ever claimed her.

Blackjackie followed me around the garden like a puppy, singing in a high-pitched meow that meant, "Pet me, pet me!" Up on the picnic table she'd climb and yowl until I sat on the bench and ran my fingers through her fur. Ten minutes would go by and she'd still be purring. If I removed my hand, she'd start begging again.

Before long I learned to take frequent breaks from weeding to pet Blackjackie, who would jump up on any bench near where I was gardening to remind me of my more important job. In the long summer evenings she'd stretch out on the patio beside my chair and contemplate the garden.

I nicknamed the blond cat from across the street Rolly for his standard greeting: rolling onto his back on the asphalt driveway where he writhed around for a while, then looked back at me in a fetching way to let me know I should scratch his tummy. When he'd had enough he would stand up, utter two high-pitched meows, and walk towards the garage. That was the signal for me to get him a handful of kibble from the container on the shelf.

One morning Rolly arrived wearing a collar with a name tag and phone number. His real name is Charlie so now I must call him Rolly Charlie. If I sit on the patio he will leap into my lap and knead and purr, shedding copious amounts of blond fur on my pants, a small price for such a friendship. Some days he will linger all afternoon, and others he will vanish quietly, most likely to visit another honored neighbor.

After strenuous forays climbing the arbor or chasing butterflies, Rolly likes to curl up on the benches beneath the grape arbor, a secret enclave where he meditates quietly on the virtues of solitude. Or perhaps he is dreaming of his next snack. Cats are so inscrutable it's hard to tell.

To Garden is Human, but to Sit, Divine

Even if something is left undone, everyone must take time to sit still and watch the leaves turn.
—Elizabeth Lawrence

I'VE NEVER BEEN VERY GOOD at sitting in my own garden. No sooner do I plop down on a bench for a minute than I spot a patch of milkweed just about to burst its seams. Or I notice some stray branches sticking up helter-skelter on the Chinese elm tree that should be pruned back, right now. Up I jump to take care of the crisis, and before I know it hours have passed, the sun has disappeared behind the neighbor's pine trees, and the warning whine of mosquitoes chases me out of the garden.

For some of us obsessed gardeners, sitting in the garden is mostly a theoretical concept. Seats are for visitors; for us, they're garden ornaments that we enjoy looking at with the fleeting thought that some day we will actually get to sit. When life is hectic and gardening takes all our free time, the sight of a hammock, for example, suggests a feeling of delicious relaxation. An inviting bench in the dappled shade of a Japanese snowbell tree is the picture of serenity, hinting at a more leisurely time that is sure to come. Some day.

But sitting in other people's gardens is another story. Garden etiquette forbids me to pluck weeds away from home, so that sitting no longer implies laziness—it's the best gift I can give my host. Sitting and gazing at their garden with admiration, or even stark green envy, is the highest compliment I can pay. Visiting gardens is a chance for me to relax, kick back, and take in all the beauty.

Best of all is a tour of gardens organized by The Hardy Plant Society of Oregon, either to gardens in the Pacific Northwest or overseas. For a delicious slice of time I get to sit on a bus with like-minded gardeners, talking about plants, and then I step into someone else's wonderland. All I have to do is look and enjoy.

Forced into idleness, I drink in the colors and textures and enjoy the diversity of plant life. I might never turn a boxwood into a topiary in my own garden, but in someone else's, I can giggle at shrubs clipped into peacocks and squirrels. Ornamental grasses and delphiniums are too much work for me, but how delightful they are to enjoy away from home where someone else does the pruning and staking.

Sitting in gardens and soaking in the beauty feels like the ultimate luxury. Although I felt a twinge of unease at first, even a little naughty, with some practice I got to love the experience. So much so that I resolved to try it at home and pretend I was a guest in my very own garden. Especially at the end of the day when my body insists that I sit, at least for a few minutes. Especially after I've stood deadheading until my legs have turned to rubber, pruned until my arms have grown weary, weeded until my back aches. That's when I stagger towards a bench and collapse with a sigh of relief.

Then I gaze with soft eyes, as if I were daydreaming, at the colors, the textures, and shapes. I look out at the garden as if it were a painting, noticing the beautiful branching patterns of the trees and the way light shimmers on the leaves. I close my eyes and listen as the grasses rustle, the chickadees sing, the bees drone, the crickets buzz. I take a deep inhalation and notice the aroma of ripe fruit, the sweet perfume of roses, the scent of cut grass and freshly-watered beds.

I've moved a bench to one end of my secret garden,

a long, narrow corridor between the giant maiden grass hedge and a mixed border of trees, shrubs, and ground covers. This low-maintenance area requires very little tending, so there's nothing to jump up for. I can sit there and look out on a scene of green and golden leaves and empty my mind of all thoughts. I sit and feel thankful for living the best life possible, in the heart of a garden.

My People

Finding My Mentors

Provide yourselves with friends as well as kin . . .
One loyal friend is worth ten thousand relatives.

—Euripides

IN MY IDEAL LIFE, I'd have been born in England and grown up gardening beside my mother.

Instead I was born in New York City, where my mother grew philodendrons on the windowsills and my father planted orange pits in little pots.

Moving to Portland in 1972 changed everything. Strolling through neighborhood gardens, I inhaled the sweet scent of daphne, lilac, and wisteria. Even the most common flowers took my breath away. Red geraniums, orange poppies, and pink peonies were all new to me, and I was smitten by their dazzling color. Even school-bus yellow broom and red clover blooming along country roads got me excited.

Completely ignorant and full of curiosity, I worried about coming to gardening so late in life—I was already thirty, and nearly everyone I met had gardened since childhood! The soil in my yard was hard as rock and gray as pewter, and I had no idea how to fix it.

How lucky for me that right next door lived my mentor-to-be, Frank Curtis. When he saw me struggling to shove a spade into that brick-hard dirt, he ran out to help. I heard a screen door slap shut, heavy footsteps, and there stood a stocky man with white hair, the ruddy face of an outdoorsman, and mischievous blue eyes. He was hauling something that looked like an ax. He put it down to shake my hand and introduce himself. I could feel the callouses on his big, rough, working hands. "This is what you need to break up that dirt," he said. "Here, give this mattock a try." He held out a tool with a dark wooden handle, lined with age. The blade was as shiny as a brand-new dime. One end of the blade was shaped like an ax, the other like a pick. I took it in my hands and lurched forward from the weight. Frank took it back.

"Here's how you use it." He swung that mattock overhead and plunged it into the soil, over and over, breaking the ground into chunks. "Now you try it," he said. I gave it a few whacks, and my face turned red. Sweat beaded my forehead. That mattock was damn heavy. My shoulders ached from the strain.

"Let me get you going." Frank proceeded to smash up that soil for another ten minutes until the bed looked like a plowed field. He brought out a metal rake for the next step. "Here's how you do it, easy as pie." He pulled the tines back and forth, then banged a few errant chunks into submission with the back of the rake. In no time he turned those clods into coffee grounds.

This was the beginning of my education as a gardener. Frank taught me everything he knew. How he made a compost pile out of grass clippings, cantaloupe rinds, and coffee grounds. How he planted tomatoes below the crown so that stronger roots would develop.

Frank's basement was a cross between a hardware store and a garden center, full of tools, lumber and fertilizer. Each rake and spade hung on its proper hook. On the green linoleum floor, overstuffed armchairs invited us to plop down while he showed me how to divide last year's humongous dahlia clumps with a freshly-sharpened knife. Then he would hand me several chunks for my own garden.

Frank taught me to add gypsum, chicken manure, and compost to my clay soil. At first I bought materials, but soon I made a compost pile just like his. I too grew tomatoes from seed, and we competed for the earliest zucchini.

In his seventies, Frank was as feisty as a much younger man, with the wisdom, experience, kindness, and perspective of a long life well lived. He was never too busy to stop what he was doing, lean on his shovel, and tell a story about his boyhood growing up on a ranch, or of his years of running a dental supply business. "We worked hard in those days, and we didn't have much, but we managed," he said. "Always remember to spend a little and save a little, and you'll be fine." I treasured his nuggets of wisdom about life as much as the gardening tips he shared so freely.

My biological grandfathers had died years before, but Frank became my true grandfather, the grandfather of my soul. He gave me a green legacy. Out in that yard, weekends and evenings, my hands became rough like Frank's. Under his wing, I grew into a gardener.

Frank Teaches Me to Grow Tomatoes

When the student is ready, the teacher appears.
—*Ancient saying*

"I guess I'm just a dirty old man, Barbara," Frank said, grinning suggestively. He was holding up a fourteen-inch-long cucumber and his face was red as a tomato, in contrast to his white hair. "I just can't help myself," he laughed.

"Well, how about this?" I said, one-upping him with a two-foot-long zucchini from my own garden.

"You haven't seen anything yet," Frank said. "Take a look at this." He marched back to his vegetable garden and I followed along. We approached his tidy row of eggplants, their glossy purple skin gleaming in the summer sun. Frank lifted one with the tip of of his finger, displaying the unusual configuration of a normally oval vegetable. Yup, it was a boy.

With a neighbor like Frank, growing vegetables was an adventure. He liked to grow a dozen different tomatoes from seed and took pride in being the first on the block with ripe ones. He marked each plant with a homemade label: Early Girl, Big Boy, Better Boy, Beefsteak, or Roma.

"These tomato vines are growing to beat the band," he said. "And notice the sexy ties." Each tomato plant was encased in a homemade wooden cage, and the stems were gently tied to the cages with strips of old nylon stockings that Frank's wife Sadie saved for just this purpose.

It was only fitting that Sadie got to savor the first tomato. "I just love to eat tomato and mayonnaise sandwiches at midnight," she confessed. Now, when I saw their kitchen light on late at night, I pictured Sadie enjoying her midnight snack. Our houses were separated by a narrow alley and it was easy to spot each other's lights, even when the shades were discreetly lowered.

There were secrets to getting tomatoes to ripen early, and one by one, Frank taught them to me. "First you have to pinch out the suckers," he said, nipping out the soft new growth in the crotches of the tomato's branches. "They don't produce any fruit," he explained. I could smell the pungent aroma of tomato foliage as he did this.

"Try it," he said, and I followed his example. Now my fingers turned yellow with tomato leaf stain, just as his had. The aroma was both repulsive and enticing at the same time, a distinctive scent I'd never smelled before.

"It's very important to water the plants every day," he went on. "Watch how I bury these old milk jugs in the ground." He dug a hole beside each plant and set a bottomless glass milk jug in the soil, leaving the rim a little above ground level. "Now I can put the hose right into this jug and send the water straight to the roots."

The next week, Frank showed me how to remove the bottom of a glass jug to make these special watering devices. We went down to Frank's basement shop, his inner sanctum that was tidier than most living rooms. Sheets of pegboard lined the walls, with plenty of tool holders and hooks for screw drivers, ice picks, paint brushes, and brooms. A collection of baby food jars held every size of nail, screw and bolt. Glass jugs, paint cans, and buckets were lined up on a long bench.

Frank selected one glass jug from his stash, then wrapped a string around it about an inch above the bottom. He tied the string tightly and plunked the jug on an old metal table. Then he lit a match, held it to the string, and let it burn until the string was black.

"We'll wait a minute for it to cool off," he said. "You'll

see how easy it is." He slid a hammer off the pegboard, held the jug by its handle, and gave the bottom a little tap. A circle of glass fell off in a clean line, and voilà, there was the perfect homemade watering well for future tomato plants. "Take this one home for yourself," he said. "Now you know how to make more of these."

That was always Frank's way, generous and kind. He gave me a fish, and also taught me to fish, no holding back.

Finding Faith

*It's intoxicating when you find someone
who fizzes with the same exuberance.*
—Mirabel Osler

IN THE SPRING OF 1979 I was browsing through *Pacific Horticulture* magazine when an article written by Faith MacKaness about her herbaceous border in Corbett, Oregon, grabbed my attention. The story was full of practical information about how she designed and planted a massive perennial border in her country garden. A few photographs of perennials with lists of the plants she was growing convinced me I had to meet her.

Looking back, I wonder how I found the guts to call this stranger, but some kind of fire was burning inside me. I was new to growing perennials, and here was an expert who was not only growing them, but combining them artistically. In the story she confessed that she was done with staking and tying and now would do things her way, "the lazy way!" Without thinking about it, I picked up the phone, called directory information, then dialed her number.

"I read your feature in *Pacific Horticulture* and love what you're doing. May I see your garden?" I asked. "I'm crazy about perennials and want to learn everything there is to know."

"Sure, come on over! How about next Wednesday?" Her voice lilted with the cadences of the South.

I drove up the Columbia River Gorge as excited as a traveler to another planet. But at first glance, my heart sank. The view from her driveway was of a hedge of tall incense cedar (which I later learned was to buffer the garden from the fierce Gorge winds) and a pale green house. But behind the house, which had once been a school, a garden stretched for acres. The jewel in the crown was the long perennial border backed by a yew hedge, just like the photograph in the magazine.

Faith was from the South and never abandoned her heritage. It would take me a while to understand the botanical Latin she pronounced with a southern inflection. I trailed behind her, scribbling phonetic versions of the plant names in a little notebook, all misspelled, but still it was a beginning. Later on I would laugh at the difference between my hieroglyphics and the correct spellings of plants like *Eryngium* and *Phlomis*.

Faith's husband Frank was British, so there was *that* accent to understand as well. He was a bit formidable, with a dry, sometimes cutting, sense of humor. But he redeemed himself by baking the most scrumptious blueberry muffins and serving them with tea whenever I visited. Frank and Faith had a huge blueberry patch, and froze the berries for year-round muffins. Frank also raised Khaki Campbell ducks and would sometimes send me home with their eggs. One huge egg was enough for a meal, and the flavor was so luscious it lingers in my memory.

I was one of many who came to learn from Faith and photograph her garden. A mass of bulbs for every season, planted beneath a birch grove, provided color year round. But it was the vast perennial border that knocked us out, flowering against the dark green yew hedge that Faith had started from tiny cuttings. Visitors came from Eugene and Salem, from Seattle and Vancouver, BC, and we all reveled in Faith's artistry.

Back then I studied about perennials in the books of Allan Bloom, Graham Stuart Thomas, and Gertrude Jekyll, but when I went to the garden center there were hardly any for sale. I left plaintive notes with a wish list for the manager, but to no avail. So visiting Faith and seeing how she grew perennials from seed was liberating. Hundreds of rusty tin cans with holes punched in the bottom for drainage stood in a homemade cold frame, with seeds from all over the world germinating in a mix of perlite and vermiculite. She showed me lists from the seed exchanges in England and Scotland. She opened my eyes to the Rock Garden Society, the Royal Horticultural Society, and the Native Plant Society.

Every fall I would find Faith sitting on a low stool out on the lawn, stripping seeds off the stems of perennials into paper bags. She dried these to share with seed exchanges. And if I looked longingly at one of her larger perennial clumps she would slice a sliver from the edge for me to take home, although sometimes she'd warn me about a plant's foibles.

"It's a pest, but it's a very nice pest," she said of *Verbena bonariensis*, which I nicknamed "the verbena from Argentina," or sometimes "the verbena from hell." Thirty years later I'm still weeding out seedlings and giving away starts to passersby who beg for it, complete with Faith's warning, which goes ignored.

Beyond being a maven of perennials, Faith was a shining example of putting first things first. Overflowing piles of garden books, plant catalogs, and seed packets obliterated her dining room table. Life was lived outdoors; housework took a back seat. What a relief to see a woman who didn't cook, with a husband who baked blueberry muffins, both of them passionate about gardening.

Herb Orange, the Great Liberator

You have to live your life according to what comforts you, not what the rest of your family thinks you ought to be doing.
—Judith Guest

NONE OF US WAS BORN knowing how to garden, but if we're interested and curious, helping hands will not only reach out, but eagerly pull us along the path. Like a filigree of roots and rhizomes running happily underground, a network of experienced gardeners await to share their wisdom.

When I was so new to plants that I didn't know the difference between a perennial and an annual, I looked for mentors everywhere. Community college seemed the obvious place to learn, yet one teacher surpassed any I'd ever experienced.

When I first called to ask about the horticulture program at Clark College in Vancouver, Washington, the department chair himself offered to give me a tour of the campus. I was tickled by his serendipitously horticultural name—Herb Orange—and couldn't wait to meet him in person.

A short, trim man with dark wavy hair, he seemed reserved until we began talking about our backgrounds. It turned out we'd both moved to the West Coast from New York City. He'd been a loyal member of the Brooklyn Botanic Gardens since childhood and a leader of the Green Guerrillas, a grassroots group of passionate urban gardeners. I'd grown up in the Bronx, and although I never gardened early in life, I'd always loved growing houseplants and fell in love with flowering perennials soon after I moved to Portland, Oregon, in 1972. I felt an instant kinship with Herb.

He taught plant identification and design, but he took us way beyond classroom education. On every semester break he reserved the college van, asked one of the older students to drive, and led us on field trips far more interesting than any lecture or slide show.

One memorable outing included nurseries in Washington and British Columbia. We toured the Carl S. English, Jr. Botanical Garden, on the grounds of the Chittenden Locks near Ballard, Washington. A landscape architect for the US Army Corps of Engineers, English spent more than forty years developing these acres filled with unusual plants from all over the world. That's where I first saw ornamental horse chestnut trees planted in a long allée, their showy red flowers blooming above the bold leaves like torches.

None of us horticultural students had much money, so Herb arranged for us to share rooms in seedy motels along the way. Sometimes we slept two to a bed, sometimes on the floor, but on those trips sleep was hardly important. One practical student brought hard-boiled eggs and homemade applesauce to save on restaurant bills. Once I woke up in the middle of the night to the sound of chewing and the smell of tuna—a young woman was munching on a sandwich she'd brought along in her backpack.

In the evenings our whole group shared a solid meal in the cheapest dive around—a smoke-filled Chinese restaurant, a run-down pizza joint—where we relived the day's adventures. Food was about as insignificant as sleep.

Minter Gardens, east of downtown Vancouver, BC, was a highlight of our trip, a show place in spring, when thousands of red tulips, yellow daffodils, and violet hyacinths blazed color from every bed. Acres of display gardens were designed to look like Holland, complete with blue and white windmills and canals. I shot rolls of film there, trying to capture the beauty and writing names of favorites in a little notebook. The following fall I added some of these bulbs to my already overstuffed garden.

Beyond these amazing adventures, Herb's biggest gift was his faith in me. I'd been considering going back to school for yet another degree. I had a master's in social work, and now I thought I'd better get yet another degree in horticulture or landscape design.

"You're a smart woman—you can do anything you want," he told me. "You have enough degrees. Just print up business cards and get started!" Those words were the perfect antidote to my mother's opinion that I was crazy to leave a secure job in social work. It was just what I needed to ignore my father's fears that I'd never earn a living as a garden designer. With Herb's encouragement, I found a graphic designer who drew up a logo for a business card. After we talked about my love for flowers, she came up with two possibilities—a white dogwood blossom and a lily, each flower framed and encircled with my business name, Creative Garden Design. I chose the lily, ordered the cards, placed an ad in the newspaper, and began a new career designing gardens.

Herb's actions were just as empowering. When I told him I'd love to design perennial borders, he blinked, then said, "How about designing a border for the campus?"

He found a place on the grounds of the college and arranged for the landscape maintenance workers to strip off the grass and till the soil. Herb asked our class to plant it as part of the curriculum. It was a chance for all of us to practice what we were learning in the classroom and see results right away!

My first step was designing the perennial border

on paper. I was so excited and yet so unskilled. Herb critiqued my first blueprint to correct the scale—drafting was never my forte. He patiently helped me understand proportions from a bird's-eye point of view. I made a second plan with a more realistic number of plants and drew up an alphabetical plant list. Then Herb bought all the plants and stored them in the campus greenhouse.

Within a few months, we were laying out a stake-and-string grid for a long, deep perennial border. As Herb and I directed traffic, dozens of students pitched in. Scurrying here and there, they carried the plants to their alloted spots, dug holes, and settled the plants into their new homes. Eventually it all came together, and by the following year the border bloomed.

When it came time for us to find work, Herb was on the job. At every class session, he'd start by announcing opportunities that came across his desk. Even when the jobs were completely out of my range he encouraged me to try them out. One that was clearly a mismatch was turf manager for a golf course. Not only was I petrified of climbing up on a riding mower, but I considered grass the lowest form of plant life. I passed on that one. He also suggested that I teach Introduction to Horticulture, but when I saw the daunting curriculum, I bowed out. It was way too scientific for me.

Only a few years later, Herb paid me the ultimate compliment. By then I was designing outdoor gardens and taking care of indoor plants for downtown offices, earning enough to pay the mortgage. I got a phone call from one of Herb's new students. "May I come talk to you about how you got started?" she asked. "Herb raved about how ingenious you've been at creating a new career."

She sat in my living room sharing her own dreams of opening a nursery. As we sipped tea and chatted, I encouraged her to go forward with her own passion. It was not long before she began working at a garden center, then moved on to begin her very own nursery, which became famous for the epimediums like 'Hot Lips', which she hybridized.

Years later, at Herb's retirement party, some of his former students, now landscapers, designers, and contractors, stood up to tell their stories about how Herb had encouraged and guided them. Herb just ate his cake and smiled modestly. As usual, he took very little credit, saying, "They did the work. I just gave them a push."

I hope he understood, deep down, how important that push was and that those of us who came to his shindig were just a fraction of the many gardeners whose lives he changed.

Running After Ed Wood

My dear, here we must run as fast as we can, just to stay in place. And if you wish to go anywhere you must run twice as fast as that.

—Lewis Carroll

I FIRST MET Ed Wood when Master Gardener program coordinator Ray McNeilan said, "There's a guy I want you to meet who knows a lot about perennials." Ray was trying to talk me into presenting a program to master gardeners about perennials, but I balked.

"I'm no expert," I said. "I'm still learning myself!"

Ray sweetened the request by offering to get Ed to share the program with me. So here was my chance to meet a *real* expert and learn more.

Ray drove to my house in his white pickup truck and took me down to Bonsai Village in Wilsonville. This was the nursery where Ed grew plants for bonsai, as well as perennials, with the help of Elmer, a tall, stooped-over man who puttered around the greenhouses at a turtle's pace.

By contrast, Ed was short and wiry, and did everything quickly—talked like an auctioneer, smoked nonstop, and walked like he was on fire. He raced around the nursery beds and greenhouses, stopping only briefly to point to a treasured primrose, a favorite bellflower, or an especially rare rhododendron with heart-shaped leaves. As he rattled off one botanical Latin name after another, puffing away on a cigarette, I ran after him, trying to keep up while scribbling in my little notebook. I wrote so fast many of my notes were illegible the first time around, but with repeated visits I eventually got the names straight.

From Ed I learned about candelabra primroses, with tiers of pink flowers encircling their tall stems, and saw how he grew them from seed. Hundred of tiny seedlings sprang up in each pot. "Just like hair on a dog's back," Ed said. Sometimes he'd grab a cluster of seedlings out of a pot, drop them into another container, shove some potting soil around them and hand the whole business to me. After a while I learned to carry plastic bags and film canisters in my pockets for the seeds he would pinch off plants to share with me. All of this he did at top speed, so I had to be ready instantly with a bag or a canister. Ed's favorite mantra was, "You should have been here last week." Last week was always the best bloom time—it was when the bloodroot opened for three days, when a favorite cyclamen was in full flower, when the fern fronds unfurled. But to me, the day I was there always had plenty of miracles. He'd show me a huge cyclamen tuber in the oak grove, one that had been growing for so many years that it was pushing itself out of the ground. His enthusiasm was contagious, and I too marveled at the long chains of flowering currant that bloomed red in spring, at the first fringe tree I'd ever seen, its small white flowers covering the branches like confetti.

Each time I met with Ed I was grateful that he was still alive. His chain smoking and manic speed scared me to death. One day he passed out in the oak grove and I ran for help. He recovered from that episode and lived for many years afterwards; I think his passion for plants carried him far.

Ed inspired me to grow many varieties of bellflowers and primroses which were perfect carpeting plants for my city garden. The small cyclamen tuber that he gave me grew to be a big daddy and propelled seeds that have grown into more cyclamen children. All together they light up my shade garden with hot pink flowers every winter. Now I too have cyclamens like his that heave themselves out of the earth.

'Edsel Wood' Japanese red pine is named after him. 'Charbonneau' miniature Canadian hemlock and 'Ryokogu Coyokyu' Japanese cedar are among the many plants he introduced to the trade. But for me, Ed's most lasting gift was his unstoppable passion for perennials that he passed on to me like a fiery torch.

Friends Live On in My Garden

From you I receive, to you I give,
together we share, and from this we live.
—Joseph and Nathan Segal

MANY OLD FRIENDS live on in my garden through the plants they've given me. Some have passed on from this earth but their memories linger. Every time I walk by the plants they gave me, I think of them with love in my heart.

The purple filbert tree that unfolds its pleated leaves every spring started out as a rooted cutting from Loie Benedict's garden. I first met Loie at a gathering of lovers of perennial in Seattle. On that June day, a dozen or so avid gardeners met on the sunporch of a private home.

Loie and I hit it off right away. Her white hair told me she was around seventy, yet her unlined face looked a lot younger. "Come see my garden any time," she said. "I'm about an hour south of here. Call me when you're on your way and I'll make sure the gate is open." I tucked the paper napkin with her phone number in my purse.

Heading home to Portland later in the week, I called Loie, meaning to visit for an hour or so. Little did I know that her garden spread over acres, and we'd be looking at plants until the sun went down.

The gate was open when I arrived, but there was no sign of Loie. Instead, a wildflower meadow greeted me—vast stretches of blue bellflowers, purple foxgloves, and some kind of yellow flowers stacked up on sturdy stems. A rustic barn stood in the distance, the paint faded to a dusty reddish-brown. Rose perfume wafted through the air and birds twittered from the branches of old apple trees.

Eventually I found Loie kneeling at the edge of a long border filled with blue and yellow irises, a gray cat perched in a patch of sun near her feet. A slender woman with white hair pinned up in a wispy bun, she reminded me of a favorite Andrew Wyeth painting, *Christina's World*.

As Loie took me through her garden, she told me the yellow flowers were Jerusalem sage and the blue bellflowers were *Campanula persicifolia*. Every so often she stopped to pick tiny strawberries that grew like groundcover throughout the beds.

"Here, try some." She held out a handful of red fruit and I took a few. They were so small, I didn't expect much, but the flavor was sweeter than any berries I'd ever tasted. "You can pick plenty more as we go along," she said.

So we wandered, nibbling berries and admiring poppies with huge petals like crepe paper, in shades of red, coral, and even pink. Every color of iris bloomed in Loie's garden—purple, yellow, ivory, and blue, some embossed with gold and others etched with lines as fine as a cat's whiskers.

I was a new gardener at that time, growing cosmos and marigolds on a small city lot, and many of Loie's treasures were new to me. But her purple filbert tree made me sigh with pleasure and stirred serious plant lust in my heart. It was my first taste of leaves as dark as merlot wine, and I couldn't stop staring with wonder.

Quick to read the envy in my eyes, Loie disappeared for a moment and returned with a spade. She searched at the base of the tree for a sucker, dug it up, wrapped it in damp paper towels and a plastic bag, and sent me home with it. In my second garden, it grew into a fifteen-foot-tall tree with beech-like leaves that contrasted gloriously with my neighbor's yellow house.

Loie also gave me my first rugosa rose. When I admired her deliciously fragrant 'Blanc Double de Coubert', with crumpled white flowers soft as satin, she excavated a section of the shrub, chopped it off at the base, wrapped it in damp newspaper, and popped it into another plastic bag.

"Plant it as soon as you get home," she said. "You can't kill it." She was so right. It rooted down and spread into a happy colony that bloomed for most of the summer. I planted it in the bed between my driveway and my neighbors' so that we could all enjoy the cloud of perfume.

By the time Loie and I had made a complete tour of her garden we could barely see the flowers—only the white and ivory ones glowed in the dusk. Swallows swooped low in graceful arcs. I figured it was so late I'd stay in a motel that night and drive home in the morning, but Loie insisted I sleep in her guest room. That evening we couldn't stop talking, sharing our love of plants, books, and philosophy.

The next morning, after Loie fixed us Earl Gray tea, oven toast, and peaches with cream, she asked if I'd drive us north to Seattle to window shop and browse at University Bookstore. On the way back to her house we stopped to pick up some groceries. "Can you stay one more night?" she asked. "I'd love to fix us some Cornish hens for dinner."

"Twist my arm!" I said. "But only if you let me pay for the groceries." That was the beginning of many visits filled with lively conversations.

The garden has the power to bring together friends of different generations. They may even live cities apart, yet connect from the heart. Geographical distance melts away when I get wind of a special place.

I'd heard a lot about Connie Hansen's Lincoln City garden on the Oregon coast, and finally got to meet her when a mutual friend drove me over. Connie was out in her damp garden in high boots, well-worn slacks, and a flannel shirt. Her weathered face told of the many sunny days in California, where she'd gardened before retiring.

Pretty soon we were admiring chalices of pure white calla lilies that thrived in moisture, along with oceans of purple irises and drifts of pink candelabra primroses. I felt comforted to see that, like me, Connie's garden was plagued by horsetail rush, but she took it in stride. "Just keep planting better stuff until you choke it out," she said. "You'll never get rid of all of it, but you can weaken it."

I returned again and again, learning about which plants would grow in my own wet clay. Following Connie's example I planted toadflax and lady's mantle, Japanese and Siberian irises, viburnums and cranesbills. I fell in love with one particular viburnum with bronze leaves and pink flowers. Many years later I found it in a nursery and bought one for my own garden—it's called 'Pink Sensation'.

These days I'm the older gardener digging up plants for newbies. When a visitor to my garden oohs and aahs over a perfect white calla lily, out comes the spade, and up pops a division. Should someone marvel over my Jerusalem sage, now thriving in most every garden bed, I tug gently on a stem until it comes loose with a bundle of healthy roots. Viburnum slips, daylily clumps, iris rhizomes, and cyclamen tubers have paraded out of this garden to root down in places I may never see. It's enough to see the smiling faces receiving their gifts.

We garden to give; we garden to receive. In the abundant garden, where a little cutting grows into a shrub, where one seed bears hundreds of tomatoes, we can't help sharing the cornucopia. If I keep giving away enough plants, maybe I too will be lucky enough to live on in other people's gardens.

When Your Inner Critic Scolds

Almost anything you do in the garden, for example weeding, is an effort to create some kind of order out of nature's tendency to run wild. There has to be a certain degree of domestication in a garden. The danger is you can so tame your garden it becomes a thing. It becomes landscaping.

—*Stanley Kunitz*

GETTING READY TO HOST an open garden is like primping for a party. Suddenly I realize it's time for a haircut, a new outfit and some dazzling accessories. Maybe this is the excuse for finding the purple waterproof parka of my dreams!

Months before the date of the open garden, I see that the garden also needs plenty of touch-up. I notice all the flaws. Daylilies are crowding up against roses; the mulberry tree's canopy is cluttered with dead wood; 'Gypsy Queen' clematis is climbing in the wrong direction. It's time to dig up that ajuga shooting long runners and rooting down in the middle of all its neighbors. I replace it with white cinquefoil, a much prettier and more restrained ground cover with gray-green leaves and white flowers. I need new plants for gaps where tragic deaths occurred over the winter, and more color, more bold leaves. More, more, more!

As the day gets closer I worry most of all about the weather. What if it pours on the day of the open garden? What if it's hot and muggy? The perfectionist in me swells up like a mushroom in a damp woodland. But just as I'm about to rip out a columbine that's leaning awkwardly over the edge of a bed, I notice a big black bumblebee dancing from flower to flower. Wait a minute! Who is this garden for?

The columbine feeds the bee, the bee pollinates the flowers, and all of it makes me happy, even if it doesn't please the blathering critic in my head who just won't shut up. I leave the columbine alone to bloom on while questions fly through my mind. Is this a showoff garden to make me look good, or is it the garden of my heart? Is it for the bees and hummingbirds to gather nectar or for some magazine's photo shoot? Am I making this garden to get oohs and ahs or to have fun and putter?

I decide that creating a garden is a delicate balance between cultivating beauty and allowing nature's wildness to remain. A perfectly manicured garden is almost an insult to the goddess Flora, whom I picture in a flowing white chiffon gown. She'd have a garland of roses in her hair, along with a few twigs and seeds. She'd never worry about the stray weed or fret over color clashes. I can see her waltzing barefoot through the garden, a little smudge of soil on her cheek, fingers stained tomato-leaf green, reveling in scent and birdsong. So what would She want from the garden? My best guess is beauty, pleasure, and happiness. When I relax and look at the garden through Flora's eyes, joy washes over me.

Visitors at the open garden actually notice and covet the stray columbines that seed themselves here and there in wild abandon. My friend Marian and her friend Helene beg me to save seed from two double columbines, a white one blooming right in the middle of a golden shrub honeysuckle, and a pink one flowering at the edge of a shady island bed. If I'd listened to that darned inner critic and removed them, my friends would have missed out.

I'm almost always surprised by which plants visitors notice at an open garden. This May, it's a little wildflower that blew in on the wind. It's only about a foot tall, with tiny pastel pink flowers that weave between other perennials like the perfect filler in a bouquet. At first I tried to contain it, but soon gave up. It's as rampant as buttercup, but a lot sweeter. "What is it?" visitor after visitor asks.

"My best guess is some kind of catchfly," I say. But even when I warn them about its weedy nature and wild origins, they still want it. When I point out how many places it's blooming, they're still determined to take some home. I get the spade and dig out a big chunk, divide it into a dozen pieces, and hand them out like party favors. It's so easy to make gardeners happy.

Other stars of that spring open garden are less aggressive. Some are even very subtle like the cutleaf alder tree, with delicate leaves and tiny white flowers. The most admired showy flower is 'Beauty of Bednall' dahlia, blooming as early as May only because I wintered it over in a huge terra-cotta pot in the greenhouse. It has nearly black dissected leaves and deep red double flowers.

People stand in front of the container worshipping the plant. This is my kind of religion.

Garden Fans from Afar, Unite!

*I had found my tribe. It felt like a family reunion for the family
I'd never really known, a homecoming at the place where
I was always meant to be but hadn't known how to find.*
—David Levithan

As I groom a few last roses in the backyard, I hear the big tour bus thundering up my street. I race to the front garden and stride down the driveway to greet my visitors. Thirty-four members of the Wisconsin Hardy Plant Society have flown here from Madison to spend five days touring Portland gardens and nurseries.

Gardeners in baseball caps and sunhats, with cameras around their necks and big smiles on their faces, pour out of the bus like happy bees. "Welcome to my garden!" I say.

The visit I've been preparing for all week—deadheading, weeding, and watering—is now in motion. I'm not dressed for photographs since I've just been gardening, but everyone insists that tour guide Edward Hasselkus and I stand in the shade together so they can capture the moment.

Hasselkus throws his arm around my shoulder, I put my arm around his waist in a cozy pose, and the group clicks away. "We've only just met. Is this a little too familiar?" I ask, laughing.

"We're gardeners! We're friends!" he says. And that's the truth. Before long the visitors and I are chatting like long-lost cousins. The love of plants brings us together as a family. Excitement builds as they recognize familiar varieties of clematis they've grown in their own gardens. "Isn't that 'Rooguchi'?" a woman asks, pointing to the shiny purple bells. A man in a Hawaiian shirt recognizes the cutleaf alder and enunciates its name in botanical Latin, *Alnus glutinosa* 'Imperialis'.

When gardeners declaim the names of their beloved plants, it's like knowing the words to a favorite Beatles song. Warm feelings arise through this shared passion. We may not know the details of one another's lives, but we recognize each other as members of the same tribe, the plant devotees. It doesn't matter that we live in different regions or that our ages range from thirty to eighty. We're all in this consuming obsession together.

"Is that your stash?" a white-haired woman asks. She points to dozens of potted trees, shrubs, and perennials sitting on the patio, which has become a holding area for plants I've collected for years. Some day I will plant them, but meanwhile I pot them up into larger and larger containers until I find just the right places for them in the garden.

"Yes, and there are some other stashes in the potting shed, and on the bench in front of the shed, too," I confess. The woman laughs with sympathetic understanding. At ease with this deep love of plants, we will never join a twelve-step group for plant addicts.

The group is most excited about my assortment of hebes, probably because they simply can't winter over in Wisconsin. It's always what you can't grow that you covet. The one they like best is 'Amy', with glossy dark leaves and purple flowers. "I tried every hebe I could get my hands on, and they all died," says a man who looks like Clark Gable without the mustache.

"It's only in the last few years, as our weather has gotten milder, that I can winter them over," I say, trying to console him. "And you never know—some year, when we least expect it, we could still get a blast of Arctic cold that wipes out all the hebes." But I silently count my blessings for living in the more temperate Pacific Northwest.

Another big hit is the flowering pomegranate, exploding with showy orange flowers. "I'm sure it's not hardy for us, but maybe I can grow it in a pot and take it in for the winter," Clark Gable says.

That's the way it goes with those of us who are mad crazy gardeners. We'll find any way to grow a plant, even if it's just for the summer. It's such a thrill to watch these bright blossoms unfurl that even where it's not hardy, gardeners will drag pots in and out of the greenhouse, the basement, the garage—whatever it takes. Many gardeners own hand trucks and bungee cords for this purpose. Some will even carefully walk heavy pots of tender plants like dahlias very slowly, rocking them from one side to the other, moving them into a greenhouse or garage each fall. Friends have told me they wrap large pots with Bubble Wrap or heavier insulation material.

I ask my guests what they can grow well in the Midwest. Daylilies are very hardy there, and so are lilacs. "You'll have to come and see our lilac collection some time," Hasselkus says.

"What I'd really love is to go on a garden tour with your group," I reply. Each year the Wisconsin Hardy Plant Society travels either overseas or to an American destination. I'm ready to hit the road with these new friends.

We're All in This Together

I find great comfort when a fellow gardener . . . says that he's killed a large number of plants or when he admits to hating his garden. Like children, gardens can be sources of great joy, guilt and pain.
—Suzanne Edison

WHEN I VISIT other people's gardens, I feel right at home as soon as they tell me their troubles. "The spotted fruit flies ruined my raspberries," Janet said, with tears in her eyes. For many years she'd shared her delicious raspberries with friends, but not this summer.

"Oh no, I'm so sorry to hear this. I remember how your grandchildren used to sell the berries out of their little red wagons," I said. Janet smiled, remembering happier days.

"Moles are ruining my new lawn! Here it is autumn and they're still throwing up those stupid hills," Linda said.

"I know, I know. They've been running through a brand-new bed I just planted. They just love to burrow through fresh soil," I said.

Sharing these sorrows brings us closer and creates an instant bond. My neighbor and gardening buddy Doug once pointed out that you can buy two plants that are identical, plant them in the same conditions, and one will thrive while the other will die. Oh, yeah, it's not always our fault! This sparked a heartfelt discussion of the frustrations of gardening. As we exchanged war stories about mysterious losses, a comfortable rapport filled the air. We were in this together.

A garden expert whom I'd placed on a very high

pedestal once confessed that he'd created a file headed Dead Plants where he listed all his fatalities. Whew, what a relief! I wasn't the only one who killed plants. And a close friend who's a much better gardener than I—she's way more scientific and pays more attention to soil preparation—mentioned she'd lost some favorite salvias. Sympathetic compassion filled my heart, replacing the envy I'd felt before.

But if you really want to be my friend, share your plants with me. Gardeners don't let their friends go home without cuttings of their favorite roses, without divisions of their choice daylilies or hostas. When you share your bounty, you live forever in your friend's garden and heart.

Many friends live on in my garden. Herb Orange, my first horticulture teacher at Clark College, showed us how to propagate fig trees from branches. We cut six-inch lengths of fig branches and packed them in horizontal stacks in a big box, covered them with damp sand, and shoved the box under the bench of a cool greenhouse. "Really, these sticks are going to turn into fig trees?" I muttered to another student in the class.

"I guess we'll wait and see," he said. "You know Herb, always the optimist."

But a few months later, we took the rooted cuttings and planted them in potting soil. Propagating was magic! That young 'Desert King' fig tree grew in my Northeast Portland garden for six years. I dug it up and took it with me when I moved to my second garden in 1986. Since then, every August and September it bears a huge crop of fruit, green on the outside, pink on the inside, and sweet as honey.

When 'Checkerboard' fuchsia begins blooming in my garden, I always think of Ron Monnier. I'd admired its striking red and white flowers when he brought it to the St. Paul Garden Club where he gave a lecture and slide show. Afterwards, he handed me the big pot bursting with color. "Here, it's yours," he said. I stood there with my mouth open.

"Wow, thank you!" I couldn't believe my luck. Because 'Checkerboard' is not fully hardy, I move it in and out of the greenhouse each year, always thinking of Ron. Each spring I repot it and refresh the soil, and it continues to thrive.

Ron's Country Gardens was a favorite destination for such a long time it's hard to accept he's no longer in Woodburn. He and his wife Debbie moved to Milton-Freewater, where he continues to hybridize. His fuchsias live on in many gardens.

Whenever I picture Carolyn Kolb I see her radiant smile. Now a designer, for many years Carolyn and her husband Larry ran Wind Dancer Nursery, specializing in ornamental grasses. I wasn't that enamored of grasses until I saw them growing at the Kolbs' Salem garden. Carolyn's enthusiasm for them was contagious. Over the years she handed me plant after plant, saying "Try it!" and before I knew it, grasses had become a big part of my garden. She gave me my first 'Little Zebra', a more modestly-growing form of zebra grass, which proved to be the perfect screen for my air conditioning unit.

Gail Austin's daylilies joined my collection of perennials starting when she and her husband Ken ran a nursery out of their backyard. Ken's warm and welcoming personality and Gail's expert attention to detail when selecting new plants made every visit to their place delightful. It didn't hurt that they always had cookies and cold drinks on the deck overlooking the colorful backyard. You could sit there and relax, taking in the beauty while deciding which daylilies to take home.

Now retired from the nursery, Gail is busy hybridizing trilliums and gave my neighbor Doug and me some three-year-old plants to try out in our gardens. Her gifts to me over the years have been many, especially some frilly ferns, and two special daylilies when Tom and I decided to get married: 'Honeymoon Suite' and 'Wedding Band'!

Toad lilies were not my cup of tea until my friend Diane gave me a few starts from her garden. By their second summer they turned out to be splendid shade plants with curiously speckled purple flowers that make me go back for a closer look every time I pass by the big apple tree they grow under. Sturdy and subtly beautiful, they've convinced me that I need more varieties, so I keep my eyes open for new cultivars.

Slugs do nibble on toad lilies, so that adds another annoyance that Diane and I can share along with complaints about moles, lacebugs, and aphids, bringing us closer yet as long-suffering but determined gardeners. If you don't have any predators in your garden and your plants are all perfect, I don't want to hear about it!

Plant Snobbery Cured by a Visit Overseas

> We most of us have a tendency to take what's native for granted and there's an element of snobbery in this. The exotic has greater appeal.
> —Christopher Lloyd

SOMETIMES I'M A BIG plant snob, looking down my nose at red geraniums and pink zinnias, at green zucchini and old-fashioned beefsteak tomatoes. In the world of gardening it's easy to get caught up in fierce competition. In some circles, growing cutting-edge plants—the variegated, white-flowering, larger leaved, more compact, and impossible-to-find varieties of rare perennials—gives you greater status. If a plant is easy to grow, forget about it. Raising finicky, exotic, and marginally hardy plants from faraway places makes you a maven.

But on an overseas garden tour, when I visited the *Kleingarten* (small community gardens) near Duisburg, Germany, I was cured of elitism in one swift awakening. Strolling along the main walkway to see the variety of little gardens that people were creating, I was struck by the liveliness and joyful atmosphere of ordinary gardens. A white-haired woman handed a bouquet of freshly cut orange zinnias to her next-door neighbor. A tall man holding a basket stood between rows of lettuce, kale, and cabbages, getting ready to harvest them. A plump woman hoeing weeds stopped briefly to smile for a photo. In another garden, stacks of stone piled high stood waiting for the gardener to lay them down as a path.

Everyday people grew food and flowers in these modest community gardens set up for apartment dwellers who lived within walking distance. They were practical and useful places without the glamour of many of the well-designed gardens and nurseries that our group visited most other days on this tour. The faces of men and women shone with happiness. They reminded me that not everyone is lucky enough to own a house with a spacious garden. That gardening is a privilege that I should get down on my creaky knees and give thanks for. That growing any green plant in soil is a great gift. That one-upmanship and gardening don't go together.

We learned more about the *Kleingarten* project when the association chair Erwin Eichholz and several of his friends invited our group into their community clubhouse and served us beer, apple cider, and coffee. He explained these gardens are run by more than fifteen thousand clubs across Germany, with more than a million people participating. At the site we visited, the land itself belonged to the city. Because it's too close to the freeway, it's not suitable for housing. Instead, over one hundred gardens grow here, each plot about eighty by fifteen feet. The rectangular plots are lined up in tidy rows with a small cottage on each site that provides running water and shelter from heat and rain. This allows a gardener to spend the day at the *Kleingarten* with a few of the comforts of home.

Depending on the value of the cottage, a *Kleingarten* can cost as much as 8,000 euros (close to 9,000 dollars) for the life of the gardener. Participants range from twenty to ninety years old, with an average age of fifty-six.

Besides being a place to garden, the *Kleingarten* is a community. The gardeners built their clubhouse together. Everyone pitches in to clip the low hedges that frame the gardens along the central path. Neighbors enjoy outdoor garden parties together and gather in the clubhouse to socialize.

I confess that I'm not much of a community gardener when it comes to schmoozing with neighbors. Personally, I like to garden in solitude with only the chirping of birds, rustling of grasses, and an occasional cat's meow punctuating the quiet. But I do love to invite groups to visit my garden when it's in its peak. Sharing the beauty—as well as the abundant grape and apple harvest—is pure pleasure. And after my visit to the friendly *Kleingarten*, I'm thinking about dropping my shovel more often when neighbors stop by.

One sunny Sunday afternoon a few months after the tour, a member of our group invited us over for a reunion. Torn by my usual compelling addiction to putter in my own garden, I resisted staying home and went visiting. The garden was gorgeous, with big fluffy plumes of pampas grass shining in the autumn sun. Ornamental purple grapevine and autumn-flowering clematis scrambled over wrought iron railings. A beautiful 'Summer Chocolate' silk tree, five times bigger than my little starter plant at home, caught my eye. I felt a familiar stab of envy threatening to spoil the afternoon. *Remember the Kleingarten and be thankful for what you have*, a little voice whispered just in time. *I will not get caught up in competition*, I silently promised myself.

Max Ehrmann's "Desiderata" says it best: "If you compare yourself with others, you may become vain and bitter, for there will always be greater and lesser persons than yourself." The same is true of gardening. If I can just remember to love what I have, without comparing, life will be so much sweeter.

The Alligator Chain Saw Massacre

> But really, many of the joys of an old garden lie in the remaking of it . . . Mastering the art of elimination may be the hardest part of gardening.
> —Joe Eck and Wayne Winterrowd

EVEN THOUGH MY HUSBAND Tom wasn't a gardener when I met him, I imagined that surely, over time, I could inspire him. I should have known better—all his passions are done with clean hands, indoors. He worked as a software engineer, plays the trumpet and keyboard, and sings like an angel. Hard to believe, but he just plain doesn't enjoy gardening.

Still, he's very helpful when it comes to anything mechanical. His gift for quickly figuring out how things work is a huge help to me. So when I read about the Alligator electric chain saw and thought it might be just what I needed for heavy pruning, I ran it by Tom. We both looked at the photos online, where it was on sale for less than half the original cost. But trying it out in person would be much more useful.

I remembered my friend Gail had an Alligator, so I called to see if we could come by for a demonstration. She agreed enthusiastically, as she was just about to cut down her Florida dogwood, which had been declining beyond all hope.

We went over one Sunday afternoon and Gail showed us how to use the big tool with bright orange handles. Like gigantic scissors, with blades like jagged teeth, the Alligator cut through thick branches in seconds. It bit into dense wood, taking down half of the dogwood's woody frame in no time at all. I flashed on how long that would have taken me with a hand saw and was sold on the tool.

Gail handed over the Alligator to Tom, who pruned a few of the thick lower limbs with ease. "This is a great tool!" he said. "Here, you try it. I think you're gonna love it."

But when I held it up to prune the next branch, my wrists ached. I felt like a wimp, as it wasn't that heavy—less than ten pounds—but still, my hands weren't strong enough. "I'm so sorry but this won't work for me," I said. "I can't hold it without stressing my wrists."

That's when Tom said the magic words. "Honey, if you buy it, I'll run it for you." I couldn't believe my ears! I was thrilled to hear this terrific offer. Maybe Tom would join me in the garden if I got the Alligator.

Sure enough, that spring, Tom and I headed out to prune my overgrown 'Desert King' fig tree, whose branches had shot up above the roof line. I pointed out the limbs I wanted removed, and he made the cuts. Working together was so satisfying. After Tom dropped the branches, I cut them into smaller pieces with my loppers, pitched them in the wheelbarrow, and moved them to the yard debris can. In less than an hour we had reduced the tree to a manageable size.

Just like Gail, I had a sick Florida dogwood in my backyard that had become an eyesore. Later on that summer, I took the plunge one afternoon and cut off the upper branches with long-handled loppers. The next morning Tom cut down the trunk with the Alligator. What a relief to have the pitiful tree out of the picture! "Could we tackle that old lilac next?" I asked Tom.

"Sure—just show me what you want taken out." As Tom cut down old woody limbs, we both heaved big chunks into the wheelbarrow. I put these in boxes on the shoulder of the road with a cardboard sign saying "Free Wood," and they disappeared within the hour. Tom stacked the thinner branches on the ground, and over the next two days I cut them into smaller pieces to take to the big compost pile at the far end of the garden.

When our work was done, we sat down for a breather, looking out at the garden together. The dahlias were in full bloom, like giant colorful lollipops, and 'Cherry Pie' rose was ablaze with hot pink flowers. I felt deliriously happy. "Working together like this is heavenly," I said.

"Well, I do like doing the manly part of the job," Tom said. "It's a powerful feeling, chomping into those lilac trunks, watching the sawdust fly."

Boy, am I glad I got that Alligator! Who would have guessed a chain saw would bring us together in the garden?

Just Say Yes: The Joys of an Open Garden

> Another [visitor] wrote, "The more times I see your garden the better it seems. It has a kind of insane passion about it . . . I fear that it will never be possible to design such a garden—it has to be loved—to be breathed like the clay that became Adam."
> —Christopher Lloyd

WHEN I GET A PHONE CALL asking to open my garden for a good cause like the Raleigh Park Garden Tour, benefiting our neighborhood school and library gardens, I just can't say no. I pray for good weather, hope the flowers will open in time, and get to work. Company is coming and it's the best incentive to weed, mulch, plant, fertilize, and groom the garden.

There's nothing like a deadline to keep me focused. I put aside all my worries about the state of the world and concentrate on the small manageable details of life in the garden, hunting down every shred of cress, dandelion, and horsetail. Watch out, slugs and snails! I'm on a mission to crush, snip, and smash. Hunting under pots and along the edges of the beds, I track down these pests before they ruin the tender new hosta leaves. I saw off dead branches, prune overgrown shrubs, and deadhead all the spent flowers. Determined to make the garden as pretty as possible, I stamp down the molehills that have sprung up overnight.

The morning of an open garden is both terrifying and exciting. No matter how many times I do this, one scary thought never fails to creep into my mind. What if nobody comes? As the starting time draws near, I find myself listening for the sound of car doors slamming shut. What sweet relief to hear those reassuring metallic thuds, followed by the music of conversation as guests slowly drift into the garden.

Women in flowery outfits, some with straw sun hats trailing colorful ribbons, saunter down the grass path. A tall man in a Hawaiian shirt walks arm-in-arm with a tiny woman bedecked in turquoise jewelry. A grandmother, walking with a cane, is accompanied by a cluster of long-haired daughters and slender granddaughters. After about an hour, what began as a leisurely series of arrivals—with plenty of time for me to greet each visitor and show them around the garden—escalates into a wild party. The crowd thickens, the questions fly, and I'm running between the front and backyards to help identify plants.

"What's the plant with the long stems and little balls along the stems, way in the back?" asks a woman in chartreuse. When she takes me there, I see that it's Jerusalem sage, or what my husband Tom named the elevator plant, in honor of the way the flowers climb up the stems. It's not in bloom yet, but the buds are distinctive and will soon open to form a ladder of yellow flowers. "Would you like a slip?" I ask.

When she nods yes, I pull out a long stem, tugging carefully in the damp soil to make sure the runner, complete with fresh sturdy roots, comes along with the stem. We go to the greenhouse for a plastic bag. "Just put it right into a pot with damp soil as soon as you get home and let it root down for awhile before you plant it in the garden," I say.

"And what are those big purple lollipops?" asks a woman in a peach sundress, pointing to 'Purple Sensation' flowering onion. We stroll over to admire them. I swear they've increased threefold since last year. This last hard winter seems to have pushed the perennials into a surge of extra vigorous growth.

A subtle avens with pale yellow nodding flowers catches the eye of a white-haired woman. I never planted it; it just appeared in the garden and found its way to the edge of a long border where it made itself at home. I've hardly noticed it this year because the showier violet irises nearby, especially the 'Chilled Wine', which are so much more compelling. But the little avens is really very sweet. I pull my trowel out of its holster and dig up a chunk for her and back we march to the greenhouse for a plastic bag. What happens during an open garden is nothing short of magic—the garden gets admired in ways I could never imagine.

"I love the way The Sunbathers are nestled in the bushes the way they are," muses a red-headed woman. "When I first started coming here they stood out a lot, but now they've become part of the garden." It's true. I hadn't really noticed how the big terra-cotta sculptures blend right in now, as if they have been here from the dawn of time. All my fretting about how they're sinking into the earth disappears with this new way of looking at them. "Nestled" is so much kinder than "drowning" to describe their evolution.

Though it has been hours, it seems like only minutes have gone by when the last visitor leaves. The quiet is startling. I realize I will have to do this again, soon—the roses are just buds right now. Mid-June should be about right for another open garden, in honor of the roses and the hydrangeas in full bloom. I can hardly wait!

Plants

Why So Many Plants?

My garden's design is driven by plants, thousands of them.
The thrill for me is watching them grow, a high surpassed only
when meeting a new one that I don't know and can grow . . .
This is something I plan to do for the rest of my life.

—Ken Druse

NO MATTER HOW MANY plants I already have, I can't resist a new one. Is this an affliction or a passion, an obsession or a blessing? Am I a plant junkie or a life-long learner?

I'd like to see this in a positive light, so here's my excuse. When I admire a plant in someone else's garden, I see it on only one day, for a few minutes. Unless I grow 'Westerland' rose myself, I'd never get to observe it in winter, when it's standing there naked without even a single leaf along its thorny stems. I'd never experience the process from sticks to flowers: first waiting for the baby leaves to unfurl, then watching as the stems fill out with tight flower buds. I'd miss the exciting moment when the buds swell and show a tiny bit of color, and the morning when one bud shyly peels back to reveal the orange petals. Never would I witness the triumphant moment when each flower explodes from the bounds of its envelope. After all this waiting, a crescendo of color and fragrance can only be mine when 'Westerland' grows in my own garden.

To enjoy pleasure like this every day, I need lots of plants, flowers for every season, interesting leaves for every day. Especially in winter, I need consolation for the gray chilly days—hellebores for color, sweet box for scent, and dwarf conifers for blue-green and golden needles. I couldn't manage without 'Charity' and 'Arthur Menzies' mahonias that bloom in January, or the hummingbirds that line up on the nearby arbor, taking turns to dive into their flowers.

For spring, there must be earliest daffodils and blue lungwort, yellow epimediums and orange avens. It wouldn't be summer without 'Lovely Fairy' roses and 'Pinky Winky' hydrangeas, without hummingbird mint and tall blue salvias. Ginkgos turn gold, white and pink anemones rise up, and blue asters light up the garden with color come fall.

I need a complex cornucopia of plant friends to commune with throughout the years. Because I'm out there over time, helping them along a bit by pruning, grooming, watering, and feeding, I'm witnessing how they grow and mature, how their nature changes over time. Even though I don't create them, I help them flourish.

Perhaps because I've never had human children, plants have even more meaning to me. They've become the children of my heart. Even in maturity they need a little tending, so I'm always connected to them. As the years fly by, this spring reminds me of springs past and this summer reverberates with memories of many summers more distant. The overlapping pleasures are familiar, yet new, each time the current season returns. Each year the perennials spread wider, the shrubs grow more robust, the trees stretch taller.

"It seems as if all plants want to grow and get larger," my husband Tom reflected one morning over breakfast. "Are there any plants that are happy to stay the same? In that way plants are like people—they always want more." Maybe it's natural to want to expand, cover more territory and have more. Maybe we learn our insatiable lust for more plants from the very plants we collect! Maybe plants *and* people want to acquire more, no matter what the consequences. So I say indulge yourself, and grow as many plants as you can take care of. Each one will teach you something about life; each one will bring you oceans of joy.

Even after forty years of gardening I still need more plants. The craving doesn't quit. If you were to look inside my mind, you would see plants. It's a wonder that little tendrils aren't sprouting from my ears. I fall asleep daydreaming about the next set of combinations to plant together, and wake up with yet another idea, one that will make me very happy. For now.

Torn Between Two Loves: Plant Lust and Beautiful Design

The pain of losing a cherished plant in a bad winter is as nothing compared to the pain of realizing that there are at least twenty-three roses that must somehow be added to the garden if life is to be more than one long agony.
—Henry Mitchell

MAYBE I'M DRIVEN by plant lust because I didn't have a garden early in life. Up until I moved to Portland in 1972, I grew only indoor plants like African violets and Swedish ivy in the milky light of a north-facing Manhattan windowsill.

My first year in Oregon, I was overwhelmed by the dazzling array of outdoor color. When dreamy drifts of flowering cherries and plums turned the city's avenues pink, my eyes grew wide with wonder. I was in a continual state of excitement at the parade of flowers as peonies, irises, roses, daylilies, and asters exploded in turn.

I filled every inch of my first small garden with flowers, tearing out every morsel of lawn. I collected every perennial I could find, never even dreaming about garden design. Thirteen years went by, until I was so desperate for more space to experiment that I moved most of my city garden to an acre of sunny land in Southwest Portland.

With experience and a better understanding of what a garden could become, gleaned from visiting well-designed places, I was no longer satisfied to stick plants in the ground willy-nilly. I couldn't put words to it at the time, but looking back, I see that I longed to create a sense of peacefulness in my new garden.

So how does a plant nerd rein in the passion for collecting plants in order to build a more composed garden? I still struggle with these two warring desires, yet here are some of the ways I have tried to mediate between them.

At first I played it safe with pastel flowers, following a garden book's advice that this would avoid color clashes. It worked for a while, and my garden became a sweet blend of pink, lavender, pale blue, buttery yellow, and creamy white. But inevitably I fell in love with bolder, more saturated colors. Like the Sirens calling to Odysseus, electric orange, lipstick red, cobalt blue, royal purple, and even brilliant yellow seduced me. How to embrace all this riveting color and still have a semblance of tranquility?

Experimenting to see what would work, I removed a lot of the pink and lavender flowers, which helped. With most of the remaining flowers intense and vibrant, the balance between them was better. I found plants with smaller flowers so that the colors were not the big splashes of phlox, peonies, and irises, but more modest dots and dabs. Instead of screaming colors vying for attention, now glimmers of orange, red, purple, and yellow sparkled amid green leaves.

Even more important I paid attention to framing the edges of beds with well-shaped leaves. In shade, I relied on heart-shaped epimedium, lobed leaves of hellebores and rosettes of saxifrage—all evergreen and hardy. In sun, I planted many avens hybrids with green, maple-shaped leaves ('Cooky', 'Mai Tai', 'Tequila Sunrise') and coral bells with dark wine and bronze leaves ('Chocolate Ruffles', 'Obsidian', 'Licorice', and 'Mahogany').

When the front lines of beds look tidy and organized, I feel more relaxed. If the edge holds together, there's room for more commotion behind it, and I can go crazy with flowering perennials without especially good foliage. In one island bed, for example, pokers and daylily hybrids cavort in a wild array of red, orange and yellow, while avens and coral bells hybrids frame them at the edge.

Even though I'd prefer to grow one of every kind of plant, the need for peacefulness convinced me to divide and propagate some favorites and plant sweeps of them on the edge. Fortunately many of the edgers just mentioned multiply easily. Sometimes even one big pot of coral bells can be separated almost immediately into divisions and grown in smaller pots until planting time.

I've become pickier about good leaves, even within the beds and borders, seeking out the succulent leaves of upright sedums like 'Matrona', 'Chocolate Drop', and 'Frosty Morn', and a few grasses for fine texture, especially 'Bowles Golden' sedge, which has held up well for many years without any fuss. With occasional dividing, I can repeat these through the garden, thus linking the beds.

Finding a way to connect beds with each other and to connect the plants within them has been the most challenging and yet the most satisfying process, one common to many art forms. It's often called *flow*. Like a symphony, where a melody repeats from time to time, golden, silver, blue-green, bronze, or burgundy foliage repeated at intervals helps unify garden beds. In a satisfying garden, you might not even notice the skillfulness of flow, but you'll likely feel at ease.

I like to think about plants as friends at a party who like each other and mingle companionably. To get the look of a relaxed gathering, I shift textures gradually, moving from small leaves to slightly larger ones and eventually to bolder foliage, and similarly, I shift tints of color gradually. Contrast makes for drama, while gradual change enhances flow.

Recently I have discovered the unifying benefit of brown leaves, including bronze, coffee-colored, orange-brown, and mahogany. These especially complement the many orange flowers that I love lately. In a planting area surrounding a new stone patio in full sun, 'Amber Jubilee' ninebark and 'Cappuccino' sedge offer brown tints, while Himalayan blueberry chimes in with bits of bronze at the tips of the green branches. Brownish-red coral bells keep the theme going, while a few libertias with gold and green in their upright leaves add a little punch. For flamboyance, I've planted orange-flowering avens along with brilliant red-orange 'Outrageous' and 'Bandit Man' daylilies.

The designer in me tries to rule, but the plant nerd keeps clamoring to add more color. How about some 'Landini' lilies tucked in there? And look, there's room for some penstemons, and don't you want to plant a few 'Rozanne' geraniums because you love that blue-violet color? The two voices keep whispering in my ear, and I do my best to listen to them both.

Fiddling with Ferns

There is something fascinating about ferns, I find.
Without flowers they captivate by their sheer
beauty of form and greenery.
—Graham Stuart Thomas

I BECAME FASCINATED with ferns in my late sixties. Frankly, the nomenclature was daunting, and by that point in my gardening life I didn't want to spend much time memorizing names like *Polystichum setiferum* 'Divisilobum', also known as the divided soft shield fern. Since I was done with teaching gardening classes, I gave myself permission to learn only common names of ferns or even (gasp!) make up names to help me remember which was which. Their beauty and grace was too compelling for me to forego the pleasure of growing them in garden, despite their tongue-twisting Latin names.

My favorite season with ferns is spring, when it's time to snip back the old fronds and wait for the new croziers to unfurl. There they sit at ground level, little hairy fists, and before long they begin to expand. This dance of the fronds takes place over several days and is magical to watch, like so many ballerinas outstretching their arms with infinite grace.

Although many ferns flaunt elegant crests and silver, burgundy and golden tints, even the plainest sword fern makes a beautiful ground cover when planted in masses, like those beneath the towering trees along the shady hillsides flanking the Sunset Highway here in Portland. In my own garden, I find them naturalized here and there in damp corners, where their leathery fronds, evergreen and indestructible, soften the base of a fence or grace the north side of my home's foundation.

My favorite fern to this day is 'Bevis', which I bought from Russell Graham when he ran a Salem, Oregon, nursery specializing in shade plants. Its Latin name is *Polystichum setiferum* 'Plumosum Bevis', which I only remember when I look at my master list of ferns in my garden. Out in the garden I simply address Bevis with great admiration, saying, *Bevis, you are the most beautiful of all ferns in my garden,* which is absolutely true. Its fronds stand so strong and look so fresh all winter that it's hard to snip them back when the new croziers are preparing to launch.

Bevis is very lacy, yet also commanding. "This is the real prize," writes John T. Mickel in *Ferns for American Gardens*. Its arching fronds taper to a delicate point like a Japanese watercolor brush, making it extremely graceful. Mine grows at the foot of the compact strawberry tree with the benefit of morning sun, afternoon shade, and plenty of moisture. Over the years it has expanded in width, but unfortunately does not produce more divisions, so I leave it alone where it shines. Recently I bought just one more Bevis to enjoy a little further along in the lower garden.

Most everyone is captivated by the Japanese painted ferns which now come splashed with silver, burgundy, mauve, and green in many different patterns. Even though I love the colors, I'm not a big fan of their floppy habit of drooping towards the ground. My favorite variety is 'Ghost', a cross between lady fern and Japanese painted fern, because its luminous, near-white fronds are more upright and less thirsty.

Two lustrous ferns delight me whenever I pass by their subtle beauty. Japanese tassel fern is dark green and glossy with arching fronds that stay under two feet tall.

Similarly shiny, the long-eared holly fern is more upright and narrow. "It looks like the fairies sprinkled silver dust on it," says Judith Jones, owner of Fancy Fronds Nursery. Both the tassel fern and the long-eared holly fern are especially welcome between hydrangeas and other shade-loving shrubs. Grown alongside larger-leaved hostas, lungworts and epimediums, their delicate texture is the perfect complement.

I am grateful to the tassel fern for solving an aesthetic concern in my garden. A generous friend gave me a Japanese maple potted up in a half whiskey barrel. I loved the tree but was not so keen on seeing the sides of the barrel. In a flash of inspiration I bought several tassel ferns and planted them all around the pot, and within a year the wood disappeared behind the wall of ferns. Now a lovely green tapestry embellishes the Japanese maple, and I'm thrilled with the results.

One of the showiest ferns in my garden also has the longest name: King of the Male Ferns. I just call it the King. The fronds are crested, just enough to make the fern extra fancy. I often stop in front of the King to worship him and let him know how much I adore his majestic beauty. Planted in front of a birdbath, his fronds rise up about three feet tall, but then just as I start to worry that he's going to crash into the bottom of the birdbath, the crests expand and the fronds arch just enough to stay below the bowl of the birdbath. The King no doubt benefits from water spilling over the edges of the birdbath after a heavy rain. They seem to be made for each other.

Distinctively different, Rochford's holly fern stands out from its lacier brethren. Amid gentler-looking hellebores and epimediums this dark green, craggy fern looks a lot like Cascade Oregon grape. It's a James Dean kind of fern, tough-looking yet charming.

Two short ferns are ideal for low ground covers at the

edge of shady sidewalk. The little hard fern stays under six inches tall and is evergreen. Easy to grow, it goes through color changes, starting out with rosy spring tints, turning brownish-green for summer and darkening to bronze in winter. The rhizomes creep to form a pleasing colony underneath shrubs or trees. Another short fern, Himalayan maidenhair unfurls pink in spring, then turns fresh green, and in autumn when the frost comes, it goes bronze. Black stems add a striking note. Only eight inches tall, Himalayan maidenhair colonizes, spreading nicely, and is easy to divide and move to new areas of damp shade.

The delicate appearance of ferns belies their strength—although I've killed plenty of perennials, I've lost only one fern, which I later learned was not hardy to my zone. Many showier plants like roses require repeated fertilizing, watering, and deadheading, while ferns ask only for a little care in spring. Just cut back last year's spent fronds and mulch around the crown with well-rotted compost or manure to keep the soil cool and moist. Or do nothing and they will still carry on, patiently waiting for a little more attention.

I have barely scratched the surface here, only mentioning a handful of my favorite ferns. To get more involved, join the Hardy Fern Foundation or The American Fern Society, and visit the Rhododendron Species Botanical Garden in Federal Way, Washington, to view their fern collection. Browse through *The Plant Lover's Guide to Ferns* by Richie Steffen and Sue Olsen, *Ferns for American Gardens* by John T. Mickel, and *The Plantfinder's Guide to Garden Ferns* by Martin Rickard. I guarantee you greater joy in your garden.

Making My Own Mistakes

*Let yourself be wrong because it will
allow you to take more chances.*
—Clare O'Donohue

I WAS WARNED about invasive plants. But did I listen?

When I spotted coltsfoot growing in a drainage ditch along the road beside Dan's garden, I decided it would be perfect perennial for my own ditch near the mailbox. "It'll spread, probably further than the ditch." Dan smiled devilishly. I imagine he knew the trouble I was getting into, but he recognized another hortaholic (a term he'd coined) and understood I would get the plants one way or another.

"I'll keep an eye on them," I promised. He generously gave me starts of two kinds, the brilliant 'Golden Palms' coltsfoot and the round-leaved Japanese coltsfoot. They spread, just as he predicted, jumping the ditch right into a mixed border. I now spend hours digging as coltsfoot romps beneath 'Mutabilis' and 'Lovely Fairy' roses. Of course everyone who walks by my garden stops to ask about these dramatic large leaves and I warn them, knowing full well that they will get some anyway. But not from me!

'Golden Palms' has had its way in the damp border at the very bottom of the garden, where it makes a dazzling show every spring. Since I've lost control of the lower garden anyway, it's actually become a useful ground cover to choke out the native horsetail rush, a way of fighting fire with fire.

Just as soon as I admired the bright yellow flowers of golden loosestrife in Ruth Kaufman's garden, she yanked a rooted stem from the clump and handed it to me. "Here, take it. It's easy," she said. Easy sounded good to me. I was just starting to develop my Southwest Portland acre, and I needed easy plants to fill in quickly. The golden loosestrife filled in, all right. I'm still culling it out from at least half a dozen beds where it's spread by runner *and* by seed.

But even if I'd been warned how invasive golden loosestrife is, you can see from these earlier follies that it wouldn't have done any good. When I like a plant I have to grow it, and I refuse to learn from other people's experiences. This seems to be human nature—we have to go right ahead and make our own mistakes, learning from them, eventually.

I never imagined that hellebores would become too much of a good thing. Early on I encouraged them to self-sow by piling shovels full of compost at the base of the plants just as soon as the seed pods formed. When they burst open, shooting black seeds onto the compost, hundreds of infant hellebores germinated and I would transplant chunks of them to other shady places in the garden that needed ground cover.

But now, decades later, the abundance of hellebores is overwhelming, and it's time to reduce their numbers to make room for the glorious ferns that bring me endless pleasure. I've become fanatic about snipping off the seedpods before they can explode. If you visit my garden, don't be surprised if I offer you a shovel full of hellebores, just like the gardeners who handed me bearded irises and cranesbills.

Sometimes I've been way too cautious, waiting forever to put a plant in the ground. The giant maiden grass, that so many folks have admired in my garden is a good example of a plant that waited in pot prison for many years. Ironically, along with Katy McFadden's sculpture of the Sunbathers, the hedge of maiden grass has become one of the garden's signatures. Most people think it's bamboo and are surprised to find out it's an ornamental grass. It makes a ten-foot-tall privacy screen between the next-to-last border and the final "secret garden" at the south end of the garden where I like to sit and listen to the sparrows trill their arias.

When I first bought giant maiden grass, I was told it would spread gradually, but not run—it would form clumps and grow tall as a hedge. But something about those powerful roots scared me. The plant looked like it would take off and get away from me in a hurry. I figured it would behave like bamboo, despite its less frightening name. So I grew it in a gallon pot, eventually moving it up to a two-gallon, and then a five-gallon container, and there it sat for five years. Finally, when I needed a tall screening plant to hide the last space in the garden, which at that time was my giant compost pile, I took a deep breath and decided to risk it. I pried the grass out of its pot, sawed it into a dozen or so pieces with a serrated knife, and planted the substantial chunks a few feet apart. After several years, a tall wall of green grass became a screen for summer, fall, and early winter. All it needs is one annual winter pruning all the way down to the ground, and up it grows, fresh and green and sturdy. The spent canes have come in handy as stakes.

In time that compost pile became so fertile it seemed like the perfect site to plant one last border, one that would be easy care. Portuguese laurels, viburnums, various red twig dogwoods, a 'Jacqueline Hillier' elm, and a few cutleaf elderberries now form a thick wall to help restrain the neighbors' blackberries and morning glory. Beneath them masses of 'Ogon' sweet flag and snowdrops make winter colorful, while a stretch of autumn-flowering sedums brightens the border in fall.

Horsetail rush, buttercup, morning glory, and blackberry fight their way through the shrubs to remind me of what grew here long before this became a garden and what will remain when I leave this place. You could say that these are the original invasives, and they're always going to shoot me a green finger, saying, "You're not the boss of us." And in between them, along come 'Golden Palms' coltsfoot, hellebores, and golden loosestrife, my very own chosen "pests."

Rocks and Roses

*There's always an end, but the end is always
the beginning of something else.*
—Henning Mankell

IT'S THE UNEXPECTED that hits me like a sledgehammer. Although it's been thirty years since that day I came home from visiting my family in New York and noticed an enormous pile of rocks standing on the side yard, I can picture it as if it were yesterday. "Oh, my God!" My mouth fell open. Then I saw that every single bed in the garden was framed with rocks. "What?!"

I was standing there in shock and disbelief when my next door neighbor strolled by to enlighten me. "Your boyfriend was here all weekend, moving all those rocks around in the heat," she said. "His t-shirt was soaked with sweat! What a devoted guy."

"Um, he's not exactly my boyfriend," I said. "I broke up with him last week." Some months back, when I was still besotted with this movie-star-handsome, muscular guy, I'd asked him if he'd build a low stone wall to frame the front garden.

"I'm not your slave," he'd sneered. He must have changed his mind, hoping mend our relationship, but these rocks were all wrong for my garden. Actually they looked like jagged teeth. This was not the low stone wall I had dreamt of. Instead, rocks sat helter-skelter as if someone had dropped them from a helicopter.

After I got over the initial shock, I thought things through. I could call and ask him to take away all the rocks. But that would mean he'd be back in my life. Or I could let everyone I knew—neighbors, friends, rock garden society members—that there were tons of free rocks for the taking.

For the next two weeks people in pickup trucks, vans, station wagons, sedans, or even pushing wheelbarrows and hand trucks moved most of those rocks out of my garden. Neighborhood culverts are still lined with those rocks, walls have been built from them, and a few of the most picturesque rocks remain here, moss-covered by now. The whole misadventure is still a powerful memory, and sometimes I still can't believe I fell for that guy. But he was *so* good looking!

Over the years I've come to appreciate rocks more and more, to the point that I'll yell, "Stop the car!" when my husband Tom and I are driving along a road littered with fallen rocks. Tom will lug a choice rock or two into the trunk and bring them home to help frame the edge of a bed. Artfully.

Beyond the rock disaster, sometimes it's my own actions that create problems in the garden. Like the time I planted a single Gallic rose in full sun and let it have its way for twenty years. No one had warned me that species roses would romp wildly underground, forming a vast colony. My younger self was obsessed with roses and convinced that roses on their own roots would be hardier and healthier than grafted ones. But I hadn't bargained for a monoculture of Gallic roses the size of a living room. It was time for me to correct my own mistake.

I began in the fall, the perfect time for digging, picking, and chopping. Each day, for an hour to two I attacked those roses with my loppers, trenching spade, and mattock. Out came prickly canes and woody roots until the area was cleared. I even sent for a second yard debris container to hold the material and stuffed each bin to the limit.

Meanwhile I collected wheelbarrow loads of my neighbors' leaves and grass clippings, plus a friend's bagged rabbit litter and coffee grounds from the neighborhood cafes. I piled these soil builders onto the emptied ground. All winter I dreamt about what to plant in this renewed bed.

"Not another bed!" said Tom, as we strolled toward the back garden on a balmy winter day. "I thought you were going to make the garden easier."

"You're so right, Honey, I am making the garden easier. Now, instead of a forest of rose canes to prune every year, I'm going to plant conifers and well-behaved evergreen shrubs!"

"Right," he said, rolling his eyes.

"I know, I'm hopeless, gotta have new plants, gotta make the garden better."

"You're passionate about your plants, just like the way I am with songs. Gotta learn yet another one and sing it better each day," he said, smiling now.

During that winter and spring I combed the nurseries for interesting conifers, both evergreen and deciduous, to form the bones of the new bed. I came home with an intriguing weeping larch which looks like a small dragon, and a weeping dawn redwood. Later on I added an assortment of dwarf hummingbird mint and a handful of perennial hibiscus hybrids for summer color. Occasional stems of the Gallic roses still sprouted, along with a few horsetail rush, and I went after them with my trenching spade. But mainly the rose was nothing but a ghost of the past.

New discouraging sorrows were clouds of ash whitefly, and evil root weevils that have sawed the edges of epimedium, seemingly overnight. But I reminded myself that it's always something: aphids, cutworms, powdery mildew, or clematis wilt. Just when I was sighing about the latest annoyance—a tribe of slugs emerging after the recent rains—a sweet perfume floated on the air. I forgot these troubles and tracked the fragrance back to 'Gulftide' holly olive standing near the patio. Its tiny white fall flowers with a scent like gardenias turned my mood joyful. Since I have many holly olives planted throughout the garden, I visited them all and inhaled their aroma, admiring their interesting evergreen foliage—cream and gold variegated, purple, some holly-like and others rounded.

As I turned the corner, I saw shell pink 'Jean May' camellia in full bloom, earlier than ever, probably due to the extra warm summer. What delightful surprises on an October afternoon, surely enough to offset the sorrows and remind me of the bigger pleasures.

True Confessions of a Garden Designer

> . . . *the gardener is a man who, with a fading plant in his hand, runs around his little garden twenty times looking for an inch of soil where nothing is growing. Yet in two days the gardener will discover that he has planted it right on top of the scarlet shoots of the evening primrose.*
>
> —Karel Capek

OCCASIONALLY I OFFERED a Saturday morning workshop called "Planning and Planting," but recently I realized the title was a complete lie. Not that I meant to deceive anyone—I just hadn't thought things through carefully enough. Now that I've had a chance to face the truth, I confess that I hardly plan my garden at all. At least not on paper, the way the garden design books show you, with lovely watercolor renderings in which each plant is in complete harmony with its neighbors. And not with a blueprint, the way landscape design classes teach you, with aerial views that only a bird can understand.

As I was showing the students how I plan a new border, reality hit me full force. There we stood near my so-called potting shed, where every inch of ground was covered by shrubs and perennials in containers. Some that I'd bought years ago as little whips were now trees, growing in five-gallon pots and sending their roots right through the drainage holes into the ground beneath them. Each fall I'd transplant them into increasingly larger containers, muttering *I'll plant you next spring. I promise.* I began hauling plants out onto the lawn and grouping them in clusters that would make pleasing compositions, when a student in green Wellingtons burst out, "You mean you buy the plants first, and then you figure out where to plant them?"

"Well, yes," I stammered, "doesn't everyone? I mean, you fall in love with a plant, and you have to have it, so you buy it and take it home with you. You can always figure out where to plant it later. How do *you* do it?"

"I think about which plants will work in the bed, and how many, and then I go shopping for them," she replied.

"Well, I'm sure that would work too, and it's probably much smarter," I said. "But for me it's like having a big box of crayons to color with. I have to have the jumbo box with hundreds of tints and shades." Besides, I thought to myself, it's not as if I have a choice. I go to a plant sale telling myself there's nothing more I need and come home with a carload of new treasures. I just can't help myself.

Love does that. It impels you beyond the bounds of reason. At one memorable plant sale I saw a newly introduced red-stemmed, shrubby dogwood, its leaves marbled with yellow, cream, pink, and burgundy. The more I stared at 'Hedgerows Gold' the more I wanted it. I imagined seeing these colors every fall, just when I dreaded the gardening season coming to an end, when I most needed a shot of heartwarming color. On cold, gray winter days, the bright red stems would cheer me up. In springtime, the newly unfurling leaves, green with yellow touches, would launch the season with pizzazz.

There was no room in my besotted brain for thoughts of where I would place this treasure. Awe, admiration, desire, and determination occupied every gray cell as I stood with one hand hovering over the pot, waiting for the announcer to declare that the sale had officially opened. Just in case you think I'm the only afflicted one, let me add that there were five more such dogwoods on the sale table, and beside each one lurked a gardener with an outstretched arm glued to the pot, waiting to claim it.

Often collecting can get out of hand, especially after a few visits to plant sales and nurseries. That's when it's time to organize the whole business into smaller harmonious groups. I like to cluster plants with compatible growing needs: shade lovers in one group, sun lovers in another, moisture lovers together, and drought-tolerant plants in another bunch. For example, I'd gone overboard collecting hydrangeas, shade-lovers that also need plenty of moisture, so I gathered them together in one corner of the lawn and added all the like-minded plants I could find—hardy fuchsias, astilbes, hostas, ferns and lungworts.

Next, I considered heights—the tallest of the bunch, hydrangeas, belonged at the back of the border, while medium-sized hardy fuchsias would form a pleasing skirt at their base. Fortunately the upright fuchsias, with smaller leaves and flowers than the rounded, bolder hydrangeas, would contrast well in texture and form. Studying the foliage shapes and textures also helped figure out the arrangement. Hostas and lungworts have rounded and tapered leaves, distinctive enough to anchor the front of the border. They'd echo the broad hydrangea leaves, but on a smaller scale, pulling things together. Ferns and astilbes with lacy leaves would spread nicely in front of the upright midborder fuchsias and contrast with the bolder hostas and lungworts holding the front line.

Some days, ideas just won't come. When I'm just not feeling the least bit creative and I know I'll probably plop things in the ground without any artistry, that's the best time to do something totally simple-minded, like some cleanup. As I rake leaves or weed, my whole being relaxes. Worries fall away like rain soaking into the soil. Eventually wonderful ideas spring into my mind, as if the sun shining on my hair had germinated some new brain cells. And then, bingo, I can see in my mind's eye how to start the next border.

The way I look at it, gardening is one big ongoing experiment. If the flowers end up clashing, I cut them for bouquets and make a note to move the plants next spring. If the borders look too busy, I mass the edges with one kind of plant to provide some unity—when the front of the bed looks organized, you can get away with murder in the middle. There's only one ingredient that I insist on, and don't ever want to go without: joy!

A Love Letter to Shrubs

How difficult it would be to compose a satisfactory garden without shrubs. Apart from the interest and beauty of their flowers, berries and leaves, their great contribution is the solidity which they add to the design. They, and they alone, are capable, if rightly placed, of dividing the garden into separate areas and thus adding surprise to its many joys.
—Graham Stuart Thomas

WHEN FLOWERING CURRANTS welcome spring with long chains of pink flowers and the twiggy branches of 'Miss Kim' lilac burst forth with fragrant lavender flowers, I breathe a sigh of relief and say a little prayer of gratitude for the deciduous shrubs. 'Magic Carpet' and 'Goldflame' spiraeas burst into life with gold leaves tipped with orange-red, and all along the arching branches of 'Summer Wine' ninebark, chocolate-brown leaves unfurl, shaped like maple leaves.

Larger shrubs add beauty while enclosing the garden to make it more private. When the golden-variegated leaves of 'Gouchaultii' red twig dogwood come to life, the road outside my dining room window disappears, along with pickup trucks and SUVs. When the dense branches of 'Onondaga' viburnum cover themselves with leaves, they hide most of the two-story house next door.

I'm grateful for shrubs that separate the garden into more intimate spaces, like the group of 'Coral Flower Carpet' roses that divides the backyard into an upper space featuring island beds and a lower area with a grape arbor and more naturalistic borders. Even after they've bloomed, oakleaf and peegee hydrangeas thicken the borders and serve as an understory, linking the tree canopy with perennials at ground level.

Leaves come in so many colors and shapes. Even green has many shades—grass-green willows, dark green sweet box, and sage green leatherleaf viburnums. Golden-leaved forms of barberry, mock orange, and shrub dogwoods, as well as variegated snowberry, andromeda, and weigela brighten the garden. Silver Monro's ragwort and 'Sutherlandii' hebe shimmer, while purple smoke bush and purple barberries add deeper tints. Leaf shapes create interesting patterns: smoke tree foliage round as coins, false spiraea incised like ferns, and larches with bright green feathery foliage.

Spring-flowering shrubs are especially showy. A parade of viburnums welcomes the season with pink and white lacecap blossoms. Purple, magenta, and white lilac panicles invite you to inhale their heavenly perfume. Even on the freeway, shrubs celebrate spring—driving is a pleasure thanks to sweeps of pink flowering currant, dazzling yellow forsythia, and blue California lilac adorning the freeway's shoulders.

Shrubs might not bloom as long as perennials or annuals, but I dress them up with summer-blooming clematis for another flush of color. I learned this trick from Ruth Kaufman, whose Cornelius garden I visited often when I was a new gardener. I discovered her garden while driving to Blooming Nursery and noticed her hand-lettered sign on the road saying "Peonies and Irises for Sale." She loved to take me around her garden, introducing me to many perennials and bulbs, especially the 'Waterlily' autumn crocus. Peacocks roamed her garden, screaming and showing off their gorgeous plumage.

"I bet you never saw a purple flowering dogwood," Ruth said on one summer visit, with a sly gleam in her eye. As we got closer I saw that she'd trained Jackman clematis up a Florida dogwood, creating the illusion of a purple dogwood. I copied her strategy, threading clematis through the branches of trees and shrubs.

The best shrubs for supporting clematis have dense, twiggy branches for the vines to twine through. A big planting hole at the base of the shrub, enriched with compost and slow- release fertilizer, will nourish the clematis. Planted on the shadier side of the shrub, the clematis roots will stay cool and damp, while the vine scrambles upwards, seeking the sun.

I pair spring-flowering shrubs with summer-blooming clematis so that the color keeps coming. Pink 'Duchess of Albany' rambles through a cutleaf elderberry, while 'Rouge Cardinal' winds its way through a purple filbert. Darkest purple 'Romantika' climbs a golden smoke bush, and 'Burma Star' with burgundy flowers makes its way up a mock orange.

Mock orange blooms for only a few weeks in late spring, but the perfume is so divine that I keep three in the garden. In winter it's a mass of twiggy, bare branches; after it blooms it's a plain green shrub. Adding summer-blooming clematis brings the shrub back to life with garlands of fresh flowers.

Early in the morning and towards evening, shrubs come alive with bird song. While I weed I love to listen to the mourning doves hoo-hoo, bush tits whistle, hummingbirds buzz, jays screech, and sparrows trill. Towhees kick through fallen leaves in the back borders, flashing their coppery feathers as they hunt for bugs.

The best bird habitat is the bed farthest from the house where I've planted a thicket of trees, shrubs, and ground cover. The dense branches of naturalized hawthorn trees on the neighbor's property, together with a tapestry of Portuguese laurel, cutleaf elderberry, viburnums, 'Baggesen's Gold' shrub honeysuckle, and 'Hidcote' St. John's wort on my side—all indestructible—make a perfect home for nesting birds. I sit on a nearby bench listening to them praise the day and give thanks for shrubs in my garden.

Plant Romance,
Name or No Name

> *In nature's presence we are all children, nothing more,*
> *and honors and names and purses lose their significance*
> *and importance and are forgotten and only the*
> *awe and marvel in our hearts remain.*
> —Luther Burbank

ON THE LAST DAY OF JUNE, a lily bloomed in my garden that was a shade of red so dark and lustrous you would have thought someone had waxed and polished it. It was growing in a pot, hiding smack in the middle of an island bed where I had tucked it in spring, way before the speedwells and gooseneck loosestrifes all around it had risen to three feet tall. Now in summer's glory, the lily was the centerpiece of a huge garden bouquet, with blue speedwells and white loosestrifes all around it.

Tiptoeing between the perennials, I reached into the pot and pulled out the label only to find that it said "dark red lily." Hmm. Then I remembered buying it at a neighborhood garden club plant sale. It was such a reasonable price that I decided to take a chance on a lily without a name. Sometimes anonymous plants become favorites in just this way.

At a church rummage sale many years ago, I found a little green vine marked "fragrant honeysuckle." I bought it and planted it, and that summer I was bowled over by the powerful perfume. The baby vine grew vigorously enough to cover a huge, old weeping willow stump in the front yard, so I dug up a runner to climb a big sunny arbor in the backyard. The yellow and white flowers waft sweet scent into the garden with the slightest breeze, overcoming me with pleasure. The aroma actually seeks me out, unlike so many flowers that I have to put my nose into to get the slightest fragrance.

Much later on, I saw it in another garden and the owner told me it was Hall's honeysuckle. Now when people ask me what it is, I can tell them and they too can search for it and get it for themselves.

Friends have given me bearded irises without names and that's okay because I only care about their vivid velvet purple, blue, and wine tints. Planted in full sun where I hardly ever water, they hold their own—even without names.

The most moving slide show I've ever seen was early in my gardening life. I'd driven up to Seattle for a study weekend put on by the Hardy Plant Society, with slide shows in the mornings and garden tours in the afternoons. On one morning a slender woman, her white hair gathered into a bun, showed image after image of flowering perennials without uttering a word. Roses just unfurling from their tender buds, poppies with crepe-paper blossoms, and lady's mantle leaves sparkling with morning dew all paraded across the screen with no names spoken. Tears filled my eyes as I watched all these beauties in heavenly silence. (What I didn't know then was that a few years later I would meet this woman again at another gathering, and that we would become good friends through the garden.)

Although gazing at plants without anyone naming them was a very evocative experience, there are times when names are essential. When I first saw 'Robin Hood' rose in a flower arrangement, the clusters of bright pink flowers made me so happy I immediately wanted a plant for my own garden. Knowing the name helped me track down a nursery that sold it, thanks to an online search.

The minute I saw 'Rooguchi' clematis, it was love at first sight. The purple pendant flowers, like little lacquered bells, were so thick and shiny I touched them to make sure they were real. Then I stood there, worshipping their beauty. Similar sparks flew when I encountered 'Betty Corning' clematis with countless little blossoms spilling down the long stems. Fortunately, when it comes to flowers, you can fall in love over and over again with no harm done.

When visitors come to my garden and ask, I'm glad to spell out botanical and common names of plants to make it easier for them to find them. Sometimes just knowing the common name isn't enough. For example, one of my favorite summer-flowering perennials is Knautia macedonica, filled with dozens of vibrant, deep-red pincushion flowers that brighten a border. But without that specific name, if all you know is that it's a pincushion flower, you might accidentally buy an annual *Scabiosa*, a similar but less hardy plant.

One afternoon when I'd opened my garden to visitors, I noticed a woman with a big red tote bag running her fingers through the foliage of golden needle evergreen. "Wow, I love it. It's so silky," she said. "What is it?"

"It's *Metasequoia* 'Gold Rush', a special form of the dawn redwood," I said. I spelled it out for her, but she just nodded her head and stood there. She didn't search for a pencil and paper in her huge tote or even pull out her phone.

My mouth fell open. Wasn't she going to write it down? I knew from experience that moments later this crucial plant name would evaporate into thin air. The woman would go to the nursery and try to describe it to a clerk, and they would wonder if she was asking for a golden 'Skylands' oriental spruce, or perhaps a golden Hinoki cypress, or maybe even a golden Spanish fir. She'd never find 'Gold Rush' and she'd be so sorry!

So please, please, if someone gives you a name, write it down. You'll be glad to have it next time you're at a nursery or a plant sale.

In my wildest dreams, I'll have so many plants I won't want or need any more. I won't care about botanical and common names; gazing at the flowers blissfully will be enough. Some day, in my dreams.

A Plant Collector's Secret

> *He resolved that he would never again let an obsession master him, not realizing that the peculiarities of our psyches are not so easily conquered and subdued. This particular resolution was doomed to failure from the start.*
>
> —Ruth Rendell

SCENTS OF CEDAR, FIR, AND SPRUCE mingled in the damp greenhouse as my gardening buddies Doug and Joy and I roamed the aisles of European Nursery in Hillsboro, looking for treasures.

"Look at me!" whispered a 'Zebrina' pine with golden-striped needles. I ran my hands through the silky branches with pleasure. "Take me home!" the pine insisted.

I remembered seeing a thirty-foot-tall 'Zebrina' years ago at Wave Hill Gardens in New York and pulled my hand away from the pine in the gallon can. There was no way I could find space for a big conifer in my garden. This one might be little now, but I'd seen the grown-up version and knew better. "Oh come on, you know you want me. You can always grow me in a pot," the pine went on. I held it up to the light and couldn't resist. I needed it like chocolate.

This is the way it is. No matter how clearly I know there's no more room for more plants, when I see a shrub like golden-leaved 'Little Honey' oakleaf hydrangea or silvery 'Kohouts Icebreaker' dwarf fir, sooner or later, I will succumb.

The first time I might resist. If the price is sky high, I might tell myself to wait until next year. Sometimes I hold out until the second time I run into the plant before I give in. But probably before I even make one full sweep of a nursery, it jumps into my cart. Especially if there are only two or three on the display table, and for sure if there's only one.

It was like that when I came across 'Mariken' ginkgo, which I'd first seen in a Dutch garden displaying many ginkgoes new to me. 'Mariken' is a dwarf, shrubby version of the ginkgo tree, with rounded fan-shaped leaves and a compact shape. There was only one plant on the nursery bench. I gasped at the price, but then I heard it calling to me. "Look how adorable I am. I cost only as much as a bag of groceries, and I'll make you happy for a lot longer." The ginkgo's pitch was right on. Besides, I was paying for the efforts of a grower, nursery employees, water, fertilizer . . . why, it was a steal!

In just this way I go home with shrubs, perennials, even trees, without the faintest idea of where to plant them. Usually I like to buy small plants and repot them into larger containers, tending them with care. That's part of the fun: watching them grow up, contemplating where they will go, daydreaming about what other plants will make good companions.

At this point, with a garden that's nearly thirty years old, bringing in new goodies means removing old ones. I dug up 'Queen of Denmark', a shrub rose that had spread far and wide, from a bed that was once sunny. Over time, a nearby silver willow planted from a gallon pot had grown so tall that it shaded the poor rose. The Queen was easy to part with, as her flowers had dwindled along with the light.

That fall, every time I saw my neighbor across the street raking leaves, I'd holler, "Let me take those off your hands." It didn't take much persuasion for her to cross the road with her wheelbarrow and dump the leaves on the empty spot where the rose had grown. After a few loads piled up, I layered them with steer manure, coffee grounds, alfalfa meal and bonemeal. I herded worms into the bed, carrying them from the lower compost pile to their new playground. Then I looked at the blank slate, staring at the soil while imagining a variety of plants that would love the shade and grow happily together. With my huge stash of potted plants, I didn't even have to shop!

I took a first stab at the layout by digging some holes, plopping some plants in them (still in their pots), then covering the pot rims with leaves. That gave me a chance to look them over for a day or two before committing. I'd included a 'Kimberley' camellia, a 'Showy Lantern' enkianthus, several golden variegated hostas and a few lacy ferns. I'd add bulbs later this fall.

Just for fun, I asked my husband Tom to take a peek too. He's not a gardener, but he has a good eye for shapes and textures. Plus it's thrilling to see him out in the garden. "Are you planning to put a little path through so people can see these plants?" Tom asked.

"Well, they'll grow taller, in time," I mumbled. But my answer was feeble—as much as I hated to admit it, he was right. Compared to the nearby enormous silver willow casting shade and an SUV-sized viburnum, these new plants might as well have been pebbles. Only the visiting neighbor cat Blondie and I would ever know they were there.

I mulled it over, stewing about alternatives all evening. I had plenty of taller hydrangeas in pots, but they wouldn't get enough moisture or enough light to bloom beneath the willow. Tom and I watched a movie that night, which distracted me from obsessing. Still, later on, as I drifted off to sleep, I thought about the unfinished project.

"Did you know you woke up at 4 a.m. talking about plants?" Tom said the next morning.

"Really? I did?"

"Yeah, you said hydrangeas would never work there, but you had a better idea."

"What was it?" I asked, hopefully.

"I can't remember, but you were muttering about plants for a long time."

I vaguely remembered this, but the details were hazy. Luckily, later that morning in the shower's mist, the dream came back. Several husky variegated boxwoods I'd started from cuttings seven years ago were waiting for a home. They could take shade, didn't need much water, and would light up the bed. The dark green camellia would go well with them. I might transplant some tough Solomon's seal and a few hardy ferns from another garden bed.

Finally after all these years, I've figured out how to design my garden more easily. From now on, I'll just sleep on it.

Plant Sale Tango

It's been proven by quite a few studies that plants are good for our psychological development. If you green an area, the rate of crime goes down. Torture victims begin to recover when they spend time outside in a garden with flowers.

—Jane Goodall

IF YOU THINK an auction is exciting, you haven't been to a big plant sale yet. Gardeners may be gentle souls who love flowers, but when it comes to acquiring new plants, they're a fiercely competitive bunch. Being the first to grow the newest variegated, double form of a cranesbill bestows status and stirs envy in the hearts of friends. Picture hundreds of gardeners under the same roof, milling around dozens of tables filled with the latest, hottest perennials, shrubs, trees and vines. Every soul is intent on getting the best buys, juggling boxes filled with treasures as they reach for just one more clematis. Can they cram it in?

Filling a shallow carton with all sizes of potted plants, not to mention vines supported by foot-tall stakes, is an art. Transporting it though a crowded hall is a skillful dance combining tai chi with the limbo. Shoppers duck under boxes held high overhead, slide sideways between each other, and maneuver between clusters of stragglers, clogging the aisles while comparing their winter disaster stories. Make like a slug and slither between browsers, or dart to your target like a hummingbird. Whatever it takes, you must fight your way past the throngs to the front lines—the tables loaded with tantalizing green matter.

To steel yourself for the contest, and win the prize

plants, make sure to keep both hands free for grabbing. Never carry a purse—it will weigh you down and swing out of control just when you need to get through a crowd. Have mercy and don't wear a backpack—they can do a lot of damage when you turn around or bend down suddenly. Instead, wear a fanny pack or a fishing vest full of useful pockets.

Be creative about hauling your booty. I've seen a luggage carrier outfitted with plastic crates, large wicker baskets, old-fashioned shopping carts, even a carton with a sturdy rope attached for dragging.

You can miss out by hesitating—grab first and analyze later. If you're not sure you want that particular lily, add it to your box anyway. You can always return it later. Don't just drop it on the floor—be courteous and take it back to the table it came from so the vendor can offer it to another customer.

Garden sales are more fun with a like-minded friend. A true buddy will carry loaded boxes to the storage area (many plant sales have a holding pen where you can leave filled boxes and continue to shop) while you keep hunting. Of course you must return the favor. Garden pals will scout the tables, keeping one another's wish lists in mind. You can each cover half the hall, then meet in the middle to share information about where the hottest plants are located.

Don't forget to eat a hearty breakfast. You may be on your feet for hours, shopping, chatting, and learning about plants. Plan to have lunch afterwards with a friend so that you can recover and wind down, especially if there's no one at home that shares your passion. To reduce plant envy, offer cuttings or future divisions.

It's smart to arrive extra early—serious shoppers line up as much as an hour before opening. Waiting in line is a chance to make new friends and get pumped about the sale. The best plants go quickly to those who get there first.

If you volunteer to help at the sale, that usually earns you early shopping privileges the morning of the event. You also get a preview of incoming plants while you help vendors unload their trucks. Volunteers are usually members of the plant society sponsoring the sale, so join up if don't already belong. The benefits go far beyond the sale—think of it as continuing education. Most plant societies host slide shows, workshops and garden tours.

Before you go to the sale, make a list of plants you're seeking, but don't let it limit you. The list is just a guideline, not a shackle. No one ever died from having too many plants. And never allow partners, spouses, friends, or curmudgeons discourage you from experimenting with new plants. If anyone grills you about how many plants you bought, don't take the bait. Give them a Mona Lisa smile and change the subject. If they persist, remind them gently of their own particular obsessions with golf or skiing.

When it comes to selecting plants, take the one with the most stems—it will grow into a huskier plant. Although plants that are flowering will tempt you, it's better to buy plants in bud. You'll have flowers to look forward to later and get to enjoy the full bloom period.

If you're not sure about the hardiness of a plant or its bloom period or height, take advantage of reference books to learn more about the plants you're taking home. Most plant sales have a table with resources to help you make wise choices. You'll also be rubbing shoulders with experts for as long as you shop, and most gardeners are only too willing to share their knowledge.

Plant sales are part of your education as a gardener, and many benefit botanical gardens, plant societies, and garden clubs. Think of buying plants as contributing to good causes. So don't hesitate—get out there and plant shop 'til you drop—it's your duty as a responsible, charitable gardener!

In Praise of Ordinary Plants

As plantspeople we are always lured by the latest selection or newly discovered species. But often these are not an improvement over the tried-and-true, rather just something interesting and different.

—Scott Ogden

WHEN I FIRST STARTED gardening, every plant was a miracle. When the pink cosmos that I grew from seed danced in the summer breezes, when the sunflower seeds that I started in paper cups turned into towering flowers, I was thrilled. My next-door neighbors, Frank and Sadie Curtis, gave me slips of cottage pinks, rooted cuttings of lacecap hydrangeas, and chunks of their dahlia tubers, none of which had names. Life was sweet.

But as the years went by and hybridizers introduced newer varieties, the excitement built. I became more intent on finding the hottest, rarest forms of ordinary plants, those with variegated leaves, double flowers and darker stems. I dug up dozens of lady's mantle which once edged my front garden with a froth of chartreuse flowers—they were just too ordinary—and replaced them with new cultivars of epimedium. Not the original, totally reliable yellow variety, but the more enticing 'Pink Champagne' and 'Cherry Tart', 'Spring Wedding' and 'Red Queen'.

Eventually, though, this enthusiastic search for more glamorous plants began feeling terribly urgent, like a strobe light flashing at the edges of my vision. I was becoming frantic to find the latest, greatest plants. But wasn't gardening a peaceful endeavor? Wasn't the garden a place to unwind, putter and even daydream? All this obsessive plant collecting made me anxious, and spoiled the pleasure I'd taken earlier in my tranquil garden retreat.

Over time, I discovered that some of the cutting-edge plants were not only more expensive, but also less vigorous. But mostly my own competitive streak was alarming. Inner voices shouted, *Is your garden good enough? If you don't get the choicest new cultivars, you'll be left in the dust!* Maybe it was time to return to a more relaxed style of gardening, to revisit the ordinary, time-tested plants: ones that held up over the years, that grew without pampering. They were like old, reliable friends that you could hang out with comfortably, without showing off.

When I stop to consider my thirty years of gardening on a wet acre once covered with buttercup and horsetail, the time-tested plants are the ones I enjoy every day. Gone are all but one of the half dozen Eucalyptus that succumbed to wet winters, but wide-spreading Persian Ironwood and narrower 'Vanessa' Persian ironwood have flourished and grown more beautiful each year. The new leaves unfold fresh green, as beautiful as beech leaves (but without the aphids that plague the beeches) and turn shades of orange and crimson each fall.

Every katsura tree I've planted has been healthy and beautiful. Each spring, heart-shaped, bronze leaves pop up along the branches like tiny valentines. By summer the leaves are blue-green, then turn gold in fall, when they also emit the delicious aroma of cotton candy!

I've always loved Japanese maples, but a wet garden is not the best place for them. So growing them in large, ceramic containers with either "feet," or bricks placed below the pot to keep the drainage holes free, has worked well. With so many choices and color changes through the seasons, some favorites are 'Fireglow', with wine-colored leaves that take sun; 'Katsura', with golden leaves turning green in summer and orange in autumn; 'Seiryu', with delicately dissected light-green leaves turning yellow and orange; and yellow-green 'Osakazuki' that brightens to glowing red in fall.

Lately I rely on evergreen shrubs with staying power. 'Charity' Oregon grape, first introduced in the 1950s, has been a happy shrub in my garden for at least fifteen years, slowly growing close to ten feet tall and spreading about five feet wide. Its dramatic, holly-like leaves are prickly, but worth the trouble when upright clusters of yellow flowers light up the winter garden and bring on the hummingbirds. Later, blue berries appear, more subtle than the flowers, but still decorative.

Camellias have taken a back seat to some of the more exotic shade-loving shrubs, but fall- and winter-blooming sasanqua camellias especially delight me. One whose label has disappeared has single white flowers with pink edges and makes a lovely espalier against a cedar fence. Spring-blooming 'Bob's Tinsie', a single red peony-form with white centers, and a neighboring single pink camellia frame the entrance to a hut with their lustrous evergreen leaves.

'Aztec Pearl' Mexican orange is so reliable that two frame a path in the side garden, their white fragrant flowers a treat in spring. And the entire tribe of holly olive, with small, fragrant, white flowers, has been a boon to the garden, whether variegated or green, holly-leaved or round-leaved.

Deciduous shrubs with colorful leaves repeat throughout the garden. Golden 'Ogon' and 'Magic Carpet' spiraea, with tints of lime, gold, orange, and burgundy add sunshine, while burgundy ninebarks like 'Center Glow' and 'Coppertina', and smoke trees like 'Royal Purple' and 'Grace' provide a punch of purple.

Selections of hosta, coral bells, epimedium, sedum and ferns make a carpet of reliable foliage and texture. If I could only grow two hostas (but thank heavens that is not my limit!) they would be blue-green 'Krossa Regal' and golden 'Stained Glass'. And 'Dolce Licorice', 'Marmalade', and 'Frosted Violet' are some favorite cultivars of coral bells.

Don't get me wrong; I still search for unusual plants. Just the other day I found myself falling in love with 'Twist' weeping larch for its quirky and intriguing shape. I sprung for 'Simple Beauty' epidemium and put 'The Giant' epimedium on my wish list for next year. But I truly appreciate the old reliables in my garden and tell them how beautiful they are, trying my best not to compare them to my newer children.

Agreeable Abelias

Abelia comes first in plant dictionaries, and in mild regions a good case can be made for similar horticultural standing for Abelia x grandiflora. It tempts fate to suggest that any plant is invulnerable to pests, diseases, poor soil . . . or the vagaries of weather, but if there is such a plant, it is this one.
—Pamela Harper

MY FIRST ADVENTURES with abelias were a perfect example of right plant, wrong place. The previous homeowners had planted several glossy abelia next to the path that ran between my neighbor Sadie's side door and the south wall of my house. Our inner-city homes stood so closely together that from my living room window I could wave to Sadie as she played solitaire at her kitchen table. Those abelias would have made a wonderful evergreen hedge in the backyard where there was plenty of space, but they were crowded along that narrow side yard. There were *three* of them and I had to prune them every few months to keep them off the sidewalk. The more I whacked, the lustier they grew, and so I was engaged in a battle instead of a love affair.

Years later I noticed those very same shrubs glowing along a suburban road where they hid the traffic from a house standing just beyond. In the late September sun their leaves took on bronze tints, and their profuse pink-flowering branches were drooping with the weight of visiting bees. I've seen abelias glowing along freeway shoulders where they thrive with very little care.

Named for Dr. Clarke Abel, who discovered Chinese abelia on a plant expedition to China in 1817, abelias have sturdy woody stems, arching branches, and shiny leaves that come to a point. Small but profuse tubular flowers in shades of white, pink, and pink-red bloom in summer and fall. When the petals drop, pink calyxes add yet another sparkle of color.

Some abelias have the added virtue of fragrance. One autumn, on a tour of French gardens, a deliciously sweet scent enticed me to the end of a long border. A large shrub smothered in white flowers held me captive as I inhaled the perfume. I went in search of the head gardener, and in the musical cadences of French, he told me it was Chinese abelia. Back home I hunted for it for a long time, which made it all the more compelling, and finally, with great relief, I found it at a specialty nursery.

Planted in blazing sun, facing west, and in less than ideal soil, it's grown four feet tall and five feet across and has flourished through extremes of cold, heat, wind, and drought. When most of the garden is on the wane, Chinese abelia opens its fragrant white flowers, holding onto them from August through November. I've trained pink, summer-blooming 'Comtesse de Bouchaud' clematis through the strong woody branches for extra color. This abelia does lose its leaves in winter, but still is very worthwhile.

I'd never heard of fragrant abelia until Roger Gossler recommended it for its perfume. It proved to be the antidote to my disappointing experiences with daphnes—they'd bloom in my garden for five or six years and then keel over and die. Every spring this abelia's pink buds open to lighter pink flowers which waft an aroma as alluring as winter daphne. Like Chinese abelia, this variety is also deciduous, with strong woody stems through which I train 'Ruutel' clematis, with vibrant, fuchsia-pink flowers.

'Kaleidoscope' is the liveliest of my abelias, with tints of green, orange, pink, and gold in the leaves. Summer flowers are white, and in fall the foliage colors turns even more vivid. I've planted it at the head of a path leading down the west side of the garden, where its dazzling color says, "Welcome!" Especially in winter, 'Kaleidoscope' warms my heart with its cheerful countenance. 'Sunshine Daydream' is a petite version of 'Kaleidoscope' with smaller leaves offering the same multicolor effect. I've placed it beside several green hebes for a punch of brilliant color to accentuate the entry to a stone patio.

Many more abelias are yours to enjoy. I've recently planted 'Rose Creek', 'Little Richard', and 'Sherwoodii' for their reputed compact shapes, and so far they're under three feet, but time will tell.

One word of caution: if you don't enjoy pruning, don't plant abelias. The arching branches tend to spring up every which way like cowlicks, which may be frustrating to folks who like a tidier plant. I don't mind spending some time pruning them after they bloom, removing some of the older woody canes, cutting out crossing branches, and eliminating any twiggy growth that jams up the plants's interior. I actually enjoy the process of pruning and think of it as sculpting. Gardeners are not only artists playing with color; we can also become sculptors. At least that's what I tell myself when I bring the pruners inside for sharpening, yet again.

it framed the shrubs and perennials behind it beautifully with its calming, silver tints. It became the perfect low hedge, better than any boxwood. By then, I had found another 'Silberlocke' that stood up straight and planted it against a cedar fence. It's especially gorgeous when it catches the winter sun, which makes the needles sparkle even brighter.

When a purple smoke tree and a Florida dogwood both succumbed to fungal disease in a prominent bed, I grieved. But sadness turned to joy when I realized I could grow more conifers in containers there. Since they were difficult to place amid flowering perennials, I could group them together in this problem bed as a collection. Of course I would also need some beautiful new containers.

Now I had a perfect reason to hunt for more conifers—and for more ceramic containers. I could hardly contain myself! Fortunately we have quite a few conifer nurseries in the outskirts of Portland, and winter visits help liven up our rainy season. Even wholesale nurseries willingly welcomed me when I'd organize my gardening group of some twenty avid gardeners to descend as a pack. Some nursery owners even gave us an informative tour.

Conifer growers around here tend to hold forth passionately about their plants, with so much detail and enthusiasm that I nearly explode with impatience for the lecture to end so I can grab some plants! After a typical tour and talk, our group would finally disperse into a buying frenzy, doing our best to wrangle politely over the rarest specimens.

After 'Silberlocke' I fell for 'Kohout's Ice Breaker', an even more radiant fir with tinier needles that recurve so strongly that the nearly-white undersides are fully displayed. 'Ice Breaker' simply glows. Slow growing, it's taken a couple of years to come into its own. Did I mention that conifers can be expensive? I tend to buy

Can't Get Enough Conifers

If one loves blue trees, they will oblige . . . if one loves golden living sculptures, they are available . . . they produce endless shades of green. Then one spring day they will amaze you with cones lighting up like red and purple lights on a Christmas tree. No other tree in nature can do that.

—Dorothy Danforth

MY FIRST ADVENTURE with conifers began when a friend took me to a nursery specializing in them. I was going only to look, not buy, but when a group of silvery 'Horstmann's Silberlocke' firs kept winking at me, I couldn't resist. I bought the smallest plant, barely a foot tall. Back home, reality came crashing in. It didn't belong in my garden at all, sigh.

Up until then, I'd been in love with flowering perennials and roses. By the time I'd discovered 'Silberlocke', my garden was an acre of island beds and borders overflowing with color, largely inspired by English cottage gardens. Where on earth could I put a conifer?

In a pot, of course, where I could enjoy it as a treasure, all on its own. I gave 'Silberlocke' a place of honor close to the house where I'd see it every day. As it developed, I repotted it into a larger, more attractive ceramic container. But surprisingly, instead of growing taller, it burgeoned sideways. I let it have its way and enjoyed its interesting asymmetrical shape.

Eventually, when 'Silberlocke' tipped over in its pot, I figured it was telling me to plant it in the ground. I placed it at the edge of a border, right along a path where the smallest sizes both out of frugality and for the great pleasure of watching these infant plants grow up.

Even though it's considered a dwarf, the 'Curly Tops' cypress that I saw in a friend's garden was more than six feet tall. Each branchlet recurved so that the impression was of a silvery-blue mass of curls. The most dynamic conifer I'd ever met, it was so adorable I couldn't live without it. I found a one-gallon plant for sale and potted it up in a black container for contrast.

I began noticing more conifers whose branches wiggled every which way, like 'Spiraliter Falcata' Japanese incense cedar with short needles in a lively shade of green. Its gracefully twisting nature makes it super appealing and so interesting to contemplate that I placed it at the edge of a bed all by itself, instead of in a group. Similarly eye-catching, 'Vercurve' white pine has longer twisted needles in bundles of five. The plant looks fluffy and friendly. When I saw it in a friend's garden, a stab of envy told me I needed one. Thus began my interest in many more dwarf white pines, twisted or not. I probably bought 'Shaggy Dog' and 'Sea Urchin' for their names, but so what! All are soothing shades of blue-green and look charming in containers.

'Louie' was my first golden white pine. I'd seen it repeatedly in at least four garden centers before I got over the sticker shock. Lusting after it was relentless, and there was no doubt that I'd succumb—it was just a matter of when. I would run my fingers through the soft golden needles, then reluctantly leave without the plant. Until finally desire triumphed over economy, and I bought it, singing "Louie Louie" all the way home.

Another favorite is the golden Spanish fir with stiff, tightly woven needles, blue-green below and yellow at the tips. Especially in winter, this fir is eye-popping and as architectural as a piece of sculpture. Intriguing for its texture, 'Tsatsumi Gold' Hinoki cypress has glittering, threadlike foliage. I fell for more varieties of Hinoki cypress including 'Nana Lutea', 'Sunny Swirl', and 'Melody'. These three need at least partial shade, for their needles burn in full sun. 'Butterball' is especially sensitive, so needs full shade to be happy.

'Butterball' led me down the path of globe-shaped dwarf conifers, and before long I had acquired 'Cannon Ball', 'Cream Ball', and 'Silverlode' threadleaf cypresses. These three ball-shaped conifers make a quirky group that tickle me every time I pass by them. Threadleaf or Sawara cypress are less costly than most dwarf conifers, so I'm more likely to impulsively spring for them. Since the first three were so affordable, I splurged on a larger 'Mr. Bowling Ball' arborvitae. I admit that like 'Louie' and 'Shaggy Dog', it might have been its name that grabbed me.

Sometimes I must have a conifer to evoke a scene from the past. Years ago, on a freezing winter day, my father and I drove over to Wave Hill, a beautiful public garden with views of the Hudson River. Whenever I visited my father in New York, our tradition was to visit Wave Hill regardless of the weather. That February day I stood in front of a mature 'Zebrina' Himalayan pine in a trance of delight, mesmerized by the shimmering tree with striped needles. I don't really have the right place for one in the ground, so I bought one for yet another container.

My father passed away in his ninety-fourth year, but 'Zebrina' lives on in my garden. As it glimmers in the winter light, memories of our many visits to Wave Hill come flooding back, especially the pleasure of that one winter day.

The Seasons

Winter Wonder

*Even though it felt like a distant dream in the biting cold,
she knew that winter would eventually be forced to retreat.
The spring rain would soften the deep frost and once
again it would loosen its grip on bulbs and roots.*

—Helene Tursten

WINTER IS KILLING ME. I ache for more time in my garden. Mornings I peer at the outdoor thermometer from the kitchen window and keep checking until it hits 50, when I can finally go outside without my fingers turning numb inside my warmest gloves. Oh, to breathe in the damp fresh air and the scent of green, growing things, to commune with the bright pink flowers of winter cyclamen and find the first white hellebore flowers sparkling above their leaves.

Meanwhile I look out the window with longing. From a distance the tall trees surrounding the garden stand like benevolent sentries, sheltering and blessing it. Sequoias, firs, and cedars point to the steel gray winter sky, which is brightening with light on a December morning. A tracery of maple and willow branches etched between the dense pyramids of conifers reminds me that spring will come, and these bare branches will be clothed once more in bright green leaves. In this winter landscape, the chartreuse lawn, bright with moss, is the cheeriest note.

But wait. Streaks of pink appear beneath the gray clouds that drift across the sky, and my heart lifts in hope that this day will warm up. From my seat near the window I see red twig dogwoods burning in the distance and the hedge of giant maiden grass behind them like a long tan curtain. A lone bird soars across the scene, landing at the top of the tallest tree to survey his domain.

Later, I venture out into the morning chill. I crave more, but even one hour in my garden revives me from my winter torpor. As still as a rock, I stand in front of 'Charity' Oregon grape and listen to the hummingbirds buzzing from the nearby cutleaf alder tree. Soon they whiz past my head and dive into the bright yellow flowers. Dozens of bush tits hiss as they flock to the same tall shrub filled with bird candy. They're less than a foot from me on the branches, tiny birds with downy feathers, flitting from branch to branch. I am in their garden, they are in mine, and we are one in wonder.

Winter Confessions

It is a healthy thing to wait. It gives you a sense of anticipation.
—Ann Patchett

IT'S SUNNY AND COLD outside, and as I sit in my office at the computer, warm as toast, out of the corner of my eye I see big leaves falling. But I'm mistaken—when I turn to look out the big picture window, these are birds. Dozens of them fly in big drifts, swooping over the garden.

At first they land on the lawn, and in the bright December sunlight I see that they're starlings, flecked with white spots. Pecking at the grass, they tug on worm after worm, feasting on the long slippery morsels as if they're slurping up a spaghetti dinner. One fat bird finds a big stash of worms and bobs his head up and down repeatedly, piercing the lawn with his sharp beak in a mad frenzy. These guys are my little thatchers, aerating the grass naturally. When they're done with these appetizers, they're off to the next destination for their second course. All at once, the whole flock lifts off and flies to the grape arbor to snack on the last of the grapes.

To make sure the birds get enough fuel in winter, I put out a suet block in a rectangular, cage-like holder that dangles just outside the dining room window. A dozen bushtits at a time will cover that block with their little gray and brown bodies, clinging to the gridded holder—right side up, upside down, and sideways, they peck at the fatty morsels laced with seeds. More birds wait their turn, perched on the arbor a few feet away. They're very cooperative and polite, no pushing or shoving, just flitting in and out of the feeding station with grace.

This view from the dining room window is the best

cat TV in the house. Gray Webster and orange Kipper perch on the garden bench I've brought indoors, just for them—it stands between the dining room table and the window. With their rumps on the bench and their front paws clutching the windowsill, they're wild with excitement, clicking their jaws.

When the bushtits tire of the suet, they fly across the front lawn to the big *Rosa glauca*, studded with abundant red hips, and feed on the rose's fruit. There's plenty for all the little birds to share.

It's only when I spot a squirrel climbing the suet feeder that I spring into action and bang on the window. But he's too smart for me—aware he's safe on the other side of the glass, he keeps wolfing down the suet. I run out the door, and from the porch yell "Get out, get out!" The squirrel bolts, while a startled passerby looks up to see me hollering. By the fear on his face, I can tell he's wondering if I'm chasing away a human intruder.

"It's just a squirrel," I tell him, sheepishly, and retreat to the warm house. I ask myself why I'm so mad at the squirrel—he needs to eat too. But he takes such big bites! If I let him have his way, all the suet will disappear and the poor birds will starve. On the other hand, I love watching the squirrels chase each other up and down the fat trunk of the sweet gum tree, race along the top of the fence, and leap from tree to tree. Arguing with myself, replaying the same old broken record, I remind myself that I have plenty more suet blocks in the garage. Just get another one out tomorrow, I tell myself. Meanwhile enjoy the great indoors and whatever you can see from the windows! Binoculars in hand, I return to my office with a hot cup of peach black tea.

It's just too darn cold and windy outside—the leaves waiting on the lawn have turned crisp and papery, impossible to rake. I'm forced to be a lazy gardener, at least for today, and the best I can do is enjoy the views from the windows. The greenhouse effect of sun pouring in fools me into thinking it's warmed up outside, but a quick peek at the outdoor thermometer tells me it's barely 25 degrees.

I root around in the drawers and find some silk thermals that I plan to layer up in some day, maybe even tomorrow. But not yet; I'm too cozy inside, watching the birds, the eucalyptus trees swaying in the wind, and silver 'Sunshine' daisy bush catching the winter light.

Let the Light Shine

> My favorite part of winter is spring. I endure
> the darkness, cold, and near complete absence
> of life and color in winter as if incarcerated . . .
> —William Cullina

IT WAS A CHILLY DECEMBER afternoon when a ruby-throated hummingbird searched among the tightly packed flower spikes of 'Arthur Menzies' Oregon grape for an open flower. To me, it looked like the buds were completely shut, but I was wrong; at the bottom of the clusters, pale yellow flowers were just beginning to loosen up and open. The little bird dipped his beak into the lowest flowers and sipped, probing over and over all across the shrub.

I could really relate to that determined hummingbird, persistently seeking what he needed to survive. Years ago, when I worked as a medical social worker, I would tiptoe out in to the dewy garden early in the morning before climbing into my car. Desperate for color, I'd force open a furry poppy bud until the orange petals unfolded. That little bit of bright color was like a transfusion that gave me enough energy to meet the day. We all need a lift, a daily dose of beauty, especially in winter when branches are bare and buds are snuggled in tightly against the cold.

That winter day I searched for the smallest patches of color and took my time gazing at them. Hot pink and pure white winter cyclamen brightened the floor of the shade garden, surrounded by heart-shaped leaves marbled with silver. The flowers were tiny but vivid and very welcome in this quiet season. Much larger, the blooms of bright pink and white sasanqua camellias dotted the evergreen branches like Christmas lights. 'Golden Sword' yucca glowed from its cobalt blue ceramic pot. Two big containers of black bamboo, with graceful canes that danced in winter's winds, held their leaves even in the biting cold.

My hunger for color was surpassed only by a craving for more light. By 4:30 p.m. or even earlier on overcast days I left the garden reluctantly, trudging back to the house with a heavy heart. How to console myself? I reminded myself that the winter solstice would be here soon. From then on, the light would increase and the garden season would come closer each day. By January, witch hazel, winter honeysuckle, hellebores and snowdrops would flower. February would bring fragrant daphnes and sweet box, even some early daffodils and blue lungwort if I was lucky and the cold wasn't too severe. From then on, it would be a steady dance of the flowers—forsythia, rhododendrons, flowering currant, and epimediums.

Looking forward lifted my mood. Meanwhile, I took pleasure in visiting nurseries, especially those with greenhouses where I could inhale the scent of green life, explore the world of dwarf conifers and broadleaved evergreens, and rub the leaves of rosemary to release the minty aroma.

Each day I still returned to the garden to do whatever I could. Moving wood chips from the big pile on the shoulder of the road to the paths came first, to warm up. Sawing off dead wood from the massive old species roses and elderly red twig dogwoods kept me moving. One day, I noticed that the old leaves of spent irises, speedwells, and daylilies were ready for clean up. Then, on my knees, pulling the last of the soggy daylily leaves out of the bed, I came across the new shoots of the giant scilla, promising blue flowers this spring, and my heart beat faster. Also, tiny gray slugs were exposed at the very edges of the bed, and I grabbed the chance to remove them. A feeling of satisfaction coursed through me as I protected my future flowers from these slimy little pests.

Some days color surprises appeared in the sky. On the way out of the grocery store on a rainy day, a double rainbow spreading across the sky woke me up to beauty.

Late one sunny afternoon the sky turned coral and blue, as vibrant as a painting. Everyone on the road jumped out of their cars and whipped out cameras and phones to capture the moment. We all stood there, transfixed, happy to be there at just the right time to witness nature's magnificence.

Return of the Light

*We hear and read a lot about the garden in winter,
but, speaking for myself, it gives me little actual pleasure.
Nearly all pleasurable thoughts are in looking forward,
in noting bulbs pushing through, the number of
dormant flower buds on shrubs and trees and so on.*
—Christopher Lloyd

I LOVE CELEBRATING the winter solstice. From then on, each day stretches out just a little longer, bringing more daylight to garden. One evening in late December, a group of us turned a bleak winter night into a festive evening by creating a solstice party. We decorated the tables with fragrant sprigs of rosemary and branches of spruce, holly and pine from our gardens. We feasted on the good earth's bounty— kale salad, roasted beets, winter squash casserole, and steaming apple cider.

Then we read poems about winter and stories about the meaning of nature's cycles. Each of us lit a white candle and said a word or two about what winter means. Voices chimed out in the candlelight: *Cold . . . dark . . . mittens . . . naked trees . . . icicles . . . baking . . . fire in the fireplace . . . wet leaves . . . skiing.* Afterwards we spoke of our hopes and dreams for the year to come. Quite a few of us longed to spend more time in our gardens, to grow more flowers and vegetables.

It's rough for a gardener to get through winter, to lose that connection with blossoms and soil, with buds and scented leaves. I'm a little embarrassed to admit that I even miss weeding and slug hunting.

Desperate for flowers, one December morning I

cruised the cut-flower display at the market, inhaling the fresh scent of white chrysanthemums and the sweet perfume of yellow freesias. I considered buying a bouquet, but I remembered my stepmother Celia's aversion to cut flowers, because they die so soon. I eyed the flowering cyclamen in their pots and the living rosemary wreaths growing in containers, but I left empty-handed.

Back home in the garden I poked around under the hellebore leaves, looking for buds. They were down there, but closed tightly against the cold. There was no sign of the sweet box shrub opening its white buds, either.

Winter is a waiting time; but I was running out of patience!

Sitting in my home office, I gazed at the December page on the wall calendar. Georgia O'Keefe's larger-than-life size pink petunias danced against a green background, radiating warm color. Many more flowers bloomed on postcards and greeting cards pushpinned to the opposite wall: voluptuous pink peonies and roses, bronze and lavender bearded iris, pastel pink lilies and satin white magnolias. I loved looking at these reminders of the flowers that would return to my garden this spring and summer, but I needed more of the real thing now!

If it weren't so windy and rainy out, I'd have driven over to Cistus Nursery on Sauvie Island to see the borders rich with evergreen eucalyptus and hopefully some winter bloom. But I was warm and cozy indoors, so I called the nursery instead. "What's blooming in your garden?" I asked. Jim Mecca tromped around in the rain and reported on his cell phone. 'Underway' and 'Winter Sun' Oregon grape were both flowering, way ahead of my 'Charity' that still refused to open its buds.

"The eucalyptus foliage and bark look great against the overcast sky," Mecca said. He was partial to the snow gum for its green, gray and cream bark and blue-green leaves, and candlebark with mahogany stems.

The Japanese cedars were also looking great.

"They're turning that bizarre purple brown," Mecca said. He was referring to the winter tints of 'Elegans' Japanese cedar. Novice gardeners have been fooled into thinking their tree was dead, but the color change is just a response to cold weather. Come spring, the foliage takes on lively green tints.

Finally I went out for a walk in the neighborhood, enjoying the dark green sweeping branches of sequoia and the blue atlas cedars. One neighbor's mass planting of Japanese aralia was still blooming with big, white, ball-shaped flowers, and at the library the golden-variegated periwinkle was shiny with raindrops.

But it was still not enough. I got in the car and drove back to the store. I bought three bouquets of flowers—a big bunch of purple irises, a mixed bouquet of white chrysanthemums, blue-green eucalyptus and red-berried St. John's wort, and the biggest arrangement of mixed alstroemeria, in tints of peach, red, and pink.

I simply must have flowers in this gray season, even if they die next week. Now I could breathe again and get through winter, at least until the hellebores begin to bloom.

Just Play

So what's the point? The point is to relax and enjoy gardening, remembering that nature is always in charge.

—Tony Avent

IN THE MOVIE *The Visitor*, a middle-aged American college professor takes piano lessons. He tries five different teachers before he finally gives up. For him, playing piano is hard work, and it's painful to watch him toil.

Later on, he meets a young man who plays African drums with great joy. One night, the professor tries tapping gingerly on the drum. The younger fellow teaches him how to hold the drum, how to play it, and they drum together. "Don't think, just play," the drummer says. A big smile lights up the professor's formerly gloomy face as he drums, at first hesitantly and little by little with more confidence. But mainly, it's with joy, with passion, and even with anger that he eventually expresses himself.

That's what gardening is for me. It's a chance to play, sometimes awkwardly, sometimes skillfully, but most of all with a heart full of feeling.

For me, the creative fun is all about conquering the wilderness and painting new pictures with plants. Actual soil preparation, digging, and planting is the sweaty part, the workout, the excuse to skip the gym. Maintaining what I've planted as the years slide by and the plants grow up is the most relaxing part—a chance to putter. Pruning and clipping, raking, and weeding, deadheading and watering—all of these soothe and calm me. Some people like to fish just to be out on the water and unwind. For me, gardening is a chance to be out in the sun, the drizzle, the breeze, and just be. No thoughts, no worries, no plans, no regrets.

One mild winter day as balmy as April, I pulled damp leaves out of the beds and flung them onto a big tarp and dragged it to the compost pile. Earthworms glistened beneath the leaves and slithered away from the bright light. As I was cleaning up I noticed the small green leaves of fall-flowering windflowers already up at ground level. Tiny green shoots had sprouted on the clematis vines, while fresh polka-dotted leaves brightened the stems of the lungworts.

It's really hard for me to cut back the ferns in late winter—their fronds still look sweet. But if I wait too long, the new ones will unfurl and get mixed up with the older ones in a big hodgepodge. So I braced myself and snipped off the old stems, and there, patiently waiting, were the furry knots of spring's greenery. All that potential, about to burst forth. What a marvelous sight!

Standing up from fern grooming, I saw that one of winter's subtlest shrubs, winter honeysuckle, had opened its tiny white flowers. I put my nose close to the blossoms and inhaled the light fragrance. Hummingbirds visit this early bloomer, dipping their needle-nosed beaks into the funnel-shaped flowers.

I went on to cut back last year's leaves on the hellebores, perennials that make winter a season to celebrate. As I snipped off the frayed foliage I enjoyed gazing at the purple, pink, wine, white, cream, and yellow flowers. Some hellebore flowers are so dark they're nearly black, while some of the white and pink ones are splashed with burgundy speckles. The contrast between light and dark colors make drifts of hellebores sparkle. I grew many of these hellebores from seed more than thirty years ago, and they've crossed with each other to produce an abundance of tints. The taller Corsican hellebores in a soothing shade of pale green also were in full bloom. Leathery jagged leaves give these plants a more curmudgeonly character.

Tiny snowdrops with nodding flowers bloomed in little groups at the edges of beds, their white petals edged with green. Some were double, some single; each had its own beauty. These are the easiest winter-flowering bulbs to grow. Nearby, hot pink cyclamen were also in bloom. Like the hellebores, they've spread around by seed and turn up here and there in the shady understory.

Even in winter there was plenty to do out in the garden and so much to enjoy. Two hours earlier my mind had scurried around in circles, worrying about this and that. Now, thanks to the garden, my mind was clear and calm, my breath was steady and deep.

You could say that gardening is my meditation practice, that the damp earth is my kneeling cushion. Out in the garden, I'm as happy as a person can be. As a matter of fact, when I went inside the house to wash up, I looked in the mirror and saw a huge beaming smile on my face, a lot like that drummer in *The Visitor* when he learned to stop thinking and just play.

Why We Love Spring the Most

> By April I am consumed with a howling lunacy . . .
> I move around the garden like an ant, delirious
> and distraught by the riotous explosion of leaf and limb.
> —Thomas Rainer

THE OTHER MORNING I was peacefully writing when I heard a raucous racket coming from outside, so loud I couldn't ignore it. Was it a pack of wild dogs? I went out expecting some catastrophe, but soon I recognized the sound of geese, honking as loud as fire engines. It took me a while to spot them, perched way up on my neighbor's roof like two monarchs surveying their kingdom. Then I got it. They were shouting, "Spring is here!"

On days like this one in February, with sunshine and clear skies, I feel like honking, too. My energy takes a quantum leap. I pull on my garden ensemble—oldest sweats, a fleece vest, slip-on Muck boots, and a belt holding Felco pruners and a Japanese knife in two holsters. Once I head out to the garden, on the best days I'm out there until the last ray of light has faded.

Warmed by the sun and blessed by the light, plants are coming back to life, and I'm coming back to life with them. It's the great return, the bursting forth of buds, of shoots, of flowers. Color is back. Red peony shoots push though the damp soil, flowering plum trees shimmer with a froth of pink blossoms, while winter hazel glows butter yellow.

In spring the air turns gentler. It feels easier to breathe. In spring, scents fills the air, adding yet another delight to our days. On my way to prune the shrub roses, I catch a whiff of sweetness and look up to see the elephant heart plum tree blooming in a cloud of white. On a walk in Northwest Portland, the delicious perfume of pink winter daphne is enough to make me delirious with pleasure. If someone ever figures out how to bottle it, they'll make a fortune.

Spring is the season of euphoria, especially on the heels of gray, wet winter. The contrast makes us as giddy as kids released from school. For gardeners, all the good stuff is ahead of us, the long unfolding of flowers starting now with daffodils and hyacinths, followed by lilacs and peonies, roses and lavender. Lilies poke their noses up, preparing to launch green stems that will bear blossoms like trumpets later this summer. Hostas erupt from their underground homes, getting ready to unfurl quilted leaves tinted green, gold, and blue. Bright green blades of daylily and cranesbill foliage remind us that soon they will bear flowers in a dazzling array. Are we there yet?!

Sowing seeds now, we look forward to fresh lettuce and spinach; we anticipate ripe tomatoes. Raspberry canes and blueberry bushes are leafing out; fig trees show subtle swellings at the leaf nodes.

Spring brings the neighbors out, too, into our front yards where we wave to each other and eventually roam over to visit and swap stories. My neighbor Doug kindly offers to let me piggyback on his order to Brent and Becky's Bulbs, the only vendor I know who sells the 'Roxy' dahlia that I've coveted ever since spotting it on a European garden tour. Only about a foot and a half tall, with vivid dark pink flowers and nearly black foliage, it looks fantastic at the edge of a border. Doug tips me off that the Lily Garden has a 30th anniversary special on several of their orienpet hybrid lilies, including 'Silk Road', a fantastic, tall lily with tints of white, pink, and crimson.

Spring is when we marvel at how much has made

it through the winter. Who would have thought those bundles of twigs looking seriously dead would leaf out? They're actually clematis vines, alive and well—'Juuli' which will bloom blue this summer and 'Petit Faucon' which will bloom purple. Who would have guessed that 'Glacier Blue' spurge, with blue-green leaves edged in cream, would carry on untouched through the cold season and would now bear cream flower spikes shaped like seahorses?

Spring is a lucky girl. We welcome her with open arms, reveling in her beauty and the promise of renewal that she offers. Every year a vision of her arriving gets us through the bleakest winter. She breathes new life into the garden, greening up the bare branches of rambling roses, hydrangeas, and spiraeas. Yes, she'll send rain along with sun and even surprise us with a sudden hail storm, but she wakes up the plants from their long winter nap, and for that alone we love her best of all the four seasons.

Spring Surprises

Stick a few alliums in the ground in the fall and voilà!
Nodding purple baseballs declare to your neighbors
that you are, indeed, a plant whisperer.
—Thomas Rainer

ON DAYS WHEN I'M GARDENING out in the rain, neighbors passing by tell me not to work so hard. I just give them my Mona Lisa smile and keep moving. Sometimes I try to convince them that I'm really having fun, but their their raised eyebrows tell me that they don't buy it. They see a woman bundled up in in a ratty fleece jacket and mud-splattered boots, wearing surgical gloves, and shoveling wood chips into a wheelbarrow. How could that be any fun? What no one can see is how euphoric I get from racing around with my wheelbarrow in the fresh air. But besides that, each day small surprises in the garden fill me with happiness.

Lately the flowering onions make me smile. They've popped up on four-foot-tall stems like giant lollipops. On a whim, I bought a box of white ones last fall and plunked the bulbs here and there, just for fun. I stuck little twigs all around them, to warn me not to dig into them by accident. Early in May, the flowering onions began blooming in the middle of an island bed near a newly planted 'Summer Chocolate' silk tree. They added instant height while the young tree took its time growing up. In the front garden, a colony of purple flowering onions bloomed for contrast beside dazzling 'Bowles Golden' grass. I wish I'd planted even more of them near the 'Golden Spirit' smoke tree for that same electric thrill of purple and yellow.

Pop-up plants bring a quirky touch to the garden. Some, like foxgloves and columbines, seed around randomly, splashing color here and there, maybe even clashing with each other, but who cares? The bees love them, wiggling their rumps as they tunnel inside the flowers for nectar. This year pink foxgloves popped up behind 'Hot Cocoa' rose, while blue, purple, and pink columbines sprinkled themselves around the edges of island beds like fairy dust.

Sometimes my gardening passions come full circle. My first adventures with bearded irises were in the 1970s. Even though I'd dug up almost all the lawn in my small city garden, I'd run out of space for more beds. When Herb Orange, my horticulture teacher and mentor, came to visit one day, I shared my frustration with him. "I want to grow so many more plants, but I've already filled up all the beds," I said.

Herb pointed to the parking strip, which was still nothing but lawn. "What about this nice sunny space?" he said. "You could take out all the grass and plant a long border."

This was way before Maurice Horn of Joy Creek Nursery had popularized "hell strips," his catchy name for curbside borders of tough, drought-tolerant plants. I worried about what the neighbors would think, but my craving for more plants won out. I stripped all the grass from that sunny parking strip and packed it with purple irises, orange daylilies, yellow tickseed, and pink peonies. It wasn't a designer's showcase, just a blast of color that made me happy. But within a few years the irises took over, so I dug them up, slid them into a wheelbarrow, and went up my street like an old-fashioned peddler, offering irises to all my neighbors.

And then, more recently, I visited a friend's garden and fell in love with bearded irises all over again. Her irises were way more flamboyant than any I'd grown in the 1970s, thanks to all the hybridizing done in the past forty years, much of it right here in Oregon. The voluptuous blossoms in shades of wine, purple, lavender, and pink made me beg for divisions. The jumbo flowers were ruffled at the edges like the fancy party dresses of my childhood.

My friend told me how drought tolerant they are—she hardly ever watered them in summer's heat, yet they thrived. I thought about several places in my garden where I watered infrequently and asked her to save whatever she was thinning out.

That fall she handed me enough divisions to plant along the sunny shoulder of the road. Three years later, right on schedule, these gifts came into their fullness. That old saying about perennials, "the first year they sleep, the second year they creep, the third year they leap" had come true. By the third year they leapt like ballerinas. Four different colors bloomed in harmony—pastel blue-violet, midnight purple, white edged in purple, and raspberry pink—each strong stem bearing at least half a dozen sweetly scented flowers.

Spring rains and wind often knock over a few stems, a perfect excuse to cut them for the house. I found a tall, sturdy vase to support the thick stems, heavy with blossoms, and plunked it on my desk. Indoors I can admire the bouquet of irises so much more closely than out in the garden, where so many other flowers compete for attention.

The spent flowers are easy to snap off. A continuing parade of new buds open and unfurl, providing so many days of delicious color and fragrance. I had enough irises to take to a potluck gathering and to cut for our mail carrier, who drives her truck by slowly to admire the garden. I feel like a billionaire when I have enough flowers to give away. It won't be long before I'll be walking up and down my street, once again peddling irises from a wheelbarrow.

Speedy is the Pace for Spring

*Did you hear that winter's over? The basil and the
carnations cannot control their laughter.*

—*Rumi*

ONE SPRING EVENING I went to a discussion about slowing down and enjoying the moment. For the hour that we sat and talked about ways to enjoy the luxurious feeling of a slower pace, I completely loved the idea and resolved to practice it.

But the very next morning, a brilliantly sunny day in March, I couldn't do it. It was impossible to slow down in the spring garden—life was quickening everywhere I looked! Overnight the naked weeping willow across the street had turned into a bright green curtain. Spears of Solomon's seal and maiden grass were bursting through the ground. Pussy willows had shed their furry caps, sprinkling the lawn with caterpillar-like confetti.

Flowers sparkled like fireworks. The 'Thundercloud' plum was a dreamy vision in pastel pink, and branches of Cornelian cherry dogwood were studded with tiny yellow blooms. Chains of creamy winter hazel blossoms danced in the breeze, while white and yellow daffodils swayed to the same beat. How could anyone slow down, surrounded by all this excitement?

Every day more was happening. At first the small noses of coltsfoot burst through the mud in the drainage ditch. Then dark pink stems bearing pale pink upright flowers appeared, like weird little bottlebrushes. Soon huge, rounded leaves unfurled and hid the ditch completely. Neighbors walking their dogs stared at these strange-looking plants. "Is it rhubarb, or zucchini?" a man with a labrador asked. I told him it was coltsfoot, that it runs underground like wildfire, and that soon I would be digging out plants that jump the ditch.

"I guess I won't ask for any starts, then, but I'll enjoy them in your yard," he said, chuckling.

Spring is the time of year when a vigilant eye is crucial, as every little seed germinates at once. I scanned the soil for hawthorn, laurel, cress, and dandelion seedlings, and yanked them out mercilessly. Love-in-a-mist had germinated a hundredfold, so I thinned the seedlings to a reasonable number. It was the same with lungwort, way too many children, so I removed most of the innocent-looking starts before they took over the entire bed and choked out the saxifrages.

Weeding is a pleasure this time of year with the earth so damp and the small intruders so yielding. One tug and small annual grasses are history; one push of the trowel and young dandelions pop out. Even buttercup, so recalcitrant in August, slips out of the soil with just a little prying.

Wild mint drives me crazy, returning every spring like a bad dream. It grows five feet tall, with stout square stems and bright pink flowers at the tips. It loves wet soil and has made itself quite at home in the soggiest places. If it didn't colonize like wildfire and bully its way through beds and borders, I might not mind it so much. But it's such a thug that each year I fight it, digging down deeply with a trenching spade and carefully picking out the thick, white roots. They're brittle as icicles, and even the tiniest remnant that snaps off and falls to earth will produce more plants. Clearly I will never win the war—a standoff is about as good as it gets.

At the same time, plants I love multiply happily in the warm, damp earth in spring. I welcome all the little snowdrop and cyclamen seedlings that spring up here and there in unexpected places. You can never have too many of these winter wonders with their earliest flowers.

Shrubs too spread into larger colonies. 'Onondaga' viburnum, with beautifully lobed leaves that unfurl with red tints, runs underground and sends up some new stems here and there. I dug up the young starts and potted them up for friends. False spiraea was running merrily underground, so I pulled out the extras and saved them for my cousins who needed some tough greenery along their fence line.

Life is so abundant this time of year, and I feel like a tough editor, refining the garden so that it shines and sparkles like a clearly written story. So much to do and never enough hours of daylight. I tell myself that there'll be plenty of time to slow down in August. Spring is a happening time!

Fleeting Beauty

Live each season as it passes;
breathe the air, drink the drink, taste the fruit . . .
—Henry David Thoreau

IN MY EARLY SUMMER garden, everything is coming and going. The tall 'Elmshorn' shrub rose is just beginning to open her magenta flowers, when smack in front of her, purple Siberian irises are fading to pale lavender tissue paper. I make a mental note to deadhead those pitiful irises and let the rose shine.

'Elsa Spaeth' clematis is losing her luster. Just last week she was a blaze of frisbee-sized blue-violet flowers, but now those blossoms have bleached out to pastel blue. Right beside her, coral 'Cornelia' and yellow 'Danae' roses are full of fresh color, putting poor 'Elsa' to shame. The once glorious 'Gauguin' tree peony, with big flamboyant coral flowers, looks like a ghost of its former self. But wait, the bright yellow candles of pineapple broom have just opened, and their fruity scent is enough to knock me over. Fresh white and yellow Spuria irises are opening while old purple Louisanas decline. The once-beautiful flowers of the pink and white lacecap viburnums have faded to an ugly brown. What kind of joke is this? Fresh and lovely one minute and hideously rusty the next.

All the flowers are coming and going. The garden, just like life, is messy and impossible to control. Moments of perfect beauty in the bud and bloom are followed by drooping petals past their prime. How can I accept and embrace the whole process? Each year it gets a smidgeon easier, but still I long for the picture to remain ever beautiful, ever fresh. Deadheading the spent flowers is a way to sustain that loveliness, but I can't keep up with the relentless pace of change. I feel breathless, a sense of urgency driving me to spin faster and faster.

In the end, the garden itself restores me to sanity. As I snip and clip, I get closer to the fragrant flowers of coral 'Westerland' rose, just opening, and pure-white mock orange blossoms. The combination of sweet rose petals and lemon-scented mock orange infuses me with joy. I nearly faint from perfume pleasure, but somehow manage to stay on my feet, slowed down and happy to be in this moment.

On the one hand, there's the garden of my imagination, perfect and complete, the garden I dream of and can see so clearly in my mind's eye. Then there's the real garden, with all its imperfections—branches dying back of verticillium wilt, leaves marred by slug bites, rose buds green with swarming aphids.

I'll never stop dreaming of the perfect garden I hope to attain—some day. If I did, I'd probably quit the whole business and take up painting. But somewhere along the line it might be easier on my mind and heart to learn to live with the browned flowers, damaged leaves, and the occasional mole hill.

I'm not the only one who loves my garden. Beetles and leaf rollers want a piece of it too, much to my dismay.

Maybe all these comings and goings of the flowers remind me too much of my own blooming and waning. Maybe my inability to keep the garden fresh and perfect is too close to the bone. My life is just as messy, full of flowering and fading, full of joys and sorrows, full of events that are beyond my control. Sometimes I think the only thing to do is to kneel down on the green blanket of grass and touch my head to the ground like the Sufis do, in the pose of ultimate surrender.

Still, every day brings new amazement along with

decay. 'Russell's Cottage Rose' has climbed to the top of the mulberry tree and has flung her canes over the branches of the neighbor's fruit tree. Way up there garlands of rosy pink flowers drip down gleefully. For several years this rose leaned against the mulberry, not quite ready to take the leap, but finally in her fifth year, up she went, galloping to the highest point and blooming all along the way.

Who knows what blaze of energy got her going now, after our terrible winter. Was this her ode to warmth, her hymn to summer after so much cold and rain? Whatever it was, those brilliant flowers took my attention away from the frayed and spent ones all around. Parts of the garden are always waning, but thankfully there's the next beautiful wave just around the corner.

The Best and the Worst of Summer Color

*Humility, that low, sweet root,
From which all heavenly virtues shoot*
—Thomas Moore

NO MATTER HOW careful I am about color combinations, all does not go as planned. Inevitably I plant a new perennial in the fall in what looks like the perfect place. But lurking underground is a dormant plant just waiting until next summer to chime in for a horrendous color clash.

A couple of years ago I planted an edging of 'Cranberry Baby' daylilies all along the driveway bed. The clumps grew quickly from small chunks I'd snitched from my husband Tom's garden, forming tidy low mounds with flowers that opened for a good six weeks. The color was somewhere between pink and red—growers call it "rosy red" or "raspberry." I'd pictured the daylilies framing the sunniest part of the bed, with winter-blooming hellebores behind them in partial shade, together with hostas and ferns for texture. All was well until neon-orange lilies popped up right behind the daylilies. Ouch! Where the heck did they come from? My best guess is that they were part of a "Mixed Color Collection" of bulbs, some irresistible deal. Note to myself: *No more bargain mixes!* Not if you're as picky about color as I am.

The commotion escalated when 'Ruutel' clematis bloomed. Nurseries describe it as "magenta red," "beetroot red," "scarlet," and "red." Let me tell you, no matter what you call that color, when 'Ruutel' bloomed with 'Cranberry Baby' and the orange lilies, I wanted to cry. In desperation I cut all the flowering stems off the orange lily, put them in a vase which I set on a small table on the deck, and breathed a sigh of relief. Kitty Blackjack promptly jumped up on the table and made a very fetching picture that would have been perfect for Halloween.

Orange is tricky, especially when it comes to bulbs that travel through the garden with a mind of their own. Crocosmias are my worst nightmare, popping up where I least want them. This year they spread out at the feet of 'Chuckles' rose, which I'd bought impulsively for its large, electric-pink flowers as much as for its cute name. I didn't pay much attention to the crocosmia foliage until the orange flowers burst open right beneath the hot pink roses. Garish would be an understatement.

I spent many hours in August's heat digging crocosmia bulbs out of the parched bed with a pick, gathering them carefully into a solid bucket so that none would escape on the way to the trash. I'm sure I missed a few crocosmia crumbs hiding deep down in the soil. They'll be back to haunt me in years to come, but hopefully in smaller numbers.

Potentilla 'Rot' is a perennial I treasure for its profuse red flowers that bloom all summer, and so is Macedonian pincushion flower with pink-red flowers that keep coming until frost. But why the pincushion flower decided to seed down right beside the red potentilla is a mystery. Perhaps it's the universe giving me the finger again, saying, "Don't be so persnickety!" Together they clash, yet I know it will be fruitless to remove the pincushion flower—it will leave behind seedlings, no matter what I do—and I love the potentilla where it is.

Despite these disasters, plenty of happier plant marriages have given me great pleasure. 'Holiday Delight' daylilies, with flamboyant orange flowers accentuated by orange-red eyes, looked smashing in front of burgundy-leaved 'Penny Lane' ninebark. At the feet of the daylilies, blue-violet 'Rozanne' geranium spread her billowing skirt as a perfect complement. Nearby, 'Summer Wine' ninebark, also with burgundy leaves, made an eye-popping picture with 'Now and Zen' daylilies. The eyezones and edges of orange 'Now and Zen' are as dark as the ninebark, resulting in a sizzling color echo.

Even though I'm partial to hot colors these days, I also fell for 'Lilting Lavender' daylily a few years ago when I saw it in full bloom at Julie Holderith's nursery, Eclectic Gardens. The oversized flowers are somewhere between pink and lavender, and the plant sends up multiple branching stems so that 'Lilting Lavender' blooms for a very long time. The division Julie sold me was so generous, I immediately divided it into several chunks and spread it around to make a long drift. In front of these pretties I planted a mass of 'Aquarelle' sedums that I'd also propagated from one mother plant. The foliage is blue-green and the flowers are dusty pink.

I love Clematis 'Rooguchi' so much that I accidentally bought it twice. (Hey, worse things can happen, like not buying it at all.) Its adorable purple flowers look like little lacquered bells, and bloom from summer into fall. Since I had two, I sent each one up a red twig dogwood. One scrambles through the pure yellow leaves of a golden red twig while the second winds its way up 'Gouchaultii' red twig with golden-variegated leaves.

A small caution—both of these red twig dogwoods would like to become trees and need ruthless pruning to stay shrubby. Two years ago I pruned 'Gouchaultii' so severely I was sure it would die, but this summer it's back just the way I like it, as a six-foot-tall shrub that screens out the traffic.

I adore avens for several excellent qualities: maple-shaped leaves that frame island beds so well; tolerance for wet soil; and a profusion of orange, yellow, and red flowers. 'Totally Tangerine' avens outdid them all, with a stellar performance for months. The flowering stems grew to two-and-a-half feet tall and spread about two feet across, with dozens of stems smothered with tiny orange flowers. It grew so lustily that I propped it upright with low, lightweight metal edgers that look like mini-fences and it carried on happily.

The excitement came to a peak when 'Totally Tangerine' bloomed together with black-purple 'Romantica' clematis and 'Golden Spirit' smoke tree, as well as purple false indigo and 'Sunningdale Yellow' pokers. By August I was sad to deadhead the last few orange flowers, but it was time for the prima donna to take a bow and exit the stage. She left behind her beautiful lobed leaves and promised to bloom again next year. Luck was on my side this time—right behind her stood beautiful 'Brother Stefan' hosta. Hiding shyly behind 'Totally Tangerine' all summer, he now had a chance to shine.

Turning with the Seasons

Light splashed this morning
on the shell-pink anemones
swaying on their tall stems;
down blue-spiked veronica
light flowed in rivulets
over the humps of the honeybees
—Stanley Kunitz

THE END OF SUMMER is a melancholy time for me. Please don't console me with visions of autumn's crisp apples or fiery autumn color lighting up the maples. I want summer to last forever!

Each day in late summer I cut brilliant red dahlias for the table and snip roses and hydrangeas for bouquets. I feast on sun-ripened tomatoes, savoring 'Sweet One Hundred' and 'Sungold' cherry varieties, each delicious in its own way. Luckily my friend Marian shares her bounty of 'Early Girl' tomatoes with me, the tastiest kind for Greek salads on hot summer days.

Now, at the end of summer, I sit down on one of the old wooden benches, unheard of earlier in the season when there was so much to weed, water, and deadhead. I rejoice in the beauty of the fuchsias with dangling bells in red, purple, and coral. All the Michaelmas daisies, pink, blue, and purple, smell so sweet when I touch them, and bring back memories of my neighbors Frank and Sadie, who gave me divisions so many years ago. Sunflowers worthy of van Gogh bloom mahogany and yellow at the top of thick, sturdy stems, while swarms of bees and tiny skipper butterflies swim through the succulent sedums.

Some afternoons I lie on the lawn and watch big white puffy clouds drift by and become a child again. When the neighbor's cat comes visiting, we sprawl on the grass together, and he purrs like a blender while I run my fingers through his orange fur.

Raccoons have left their calling cards on the ground below the sweet gum tree, and I picture the masked thieves sitting up on the stout branches at night, gorging on figs from the nearby 'Desert King' tree.

I want to hold onto summer with both hands and never let go. I don't want this sensual season to end. I love to feel the sun warm my hair and breathe the scent of butterfly bushes drifting through the air. On some hot summer afternoons I sit quietly on the garden bench, painted purple, that is tucked into a bed in the shade of the cherry tree. I listen to the breeze ripple through the giant maiden grass, to the cry of the chickadees, to the buzz of hummingbirds zooming down from the top of the apple tree for a sip of fuchsia nectar. I bite into a ripe fig dripping with honey and want summer to last forever.

Maybe it's because I wait for summer for so long, through the rainy winter and drizzly spring, that I love it so much and cling to it so hard. Anticipation of summer carries me through the gray, cold days of February, and when it finally arrives, I want summer to last without end. But continual small signs force me to face the change of seasons. When the daylily foliage fades and I pull out the dead leaves, when the hosta leaves turn white and papery, I can't deny that summer's perennials are saying farewell, for now. Each day darkness falls a little earlier, and I smell a chill in the air. Little by little all the luscious nectarines, peaches and melons disappear from the markets. Summer is such a juicy time that it's hard to say goodbye.

Yet when fall's windflowers open their round white petals, and tiny pink cyclamen bloom, I remember that autumn brings its own pleasures. When the purple smoke tree turns orange and the katsura trees smell of cotton candy, I know fall is here to stay.

I simply can't stop the seasons from turning. Slowly and reluctantly, I must make the shift from summer to fall, no matter how much I want to resist. It's like this every year, no matter how strongly I protest. Summer's lush exuberance turns to fall's unique beauty. Crab apple trees suddenly come to life, studded with fruit turned golden, while red berries glisten in the branches of the viburnums.

Autumn sweeps me off my feet the morning the porcelain berry vine shows its colors. Like a giant's necklace, long chains of turquoise and purple beads dangle from the branches of the big purple filbert tree. All summer long the porcelain berry vine has been climbing, stretching longer and higher, flowering and forming green fruit, nearly invisible in the filbert's branches. But now in autumn, it colors up and comes to life, as beautiful as iridescent opals.

Ornamental grasses send up tall inflorescences in fall, especially my hedge of giant maiden grass, now topped with cream-colored plumes. And when the ginkgo leaves turn luminous yellow and the parrotia tree glows orange and gold, I have to admit that fall is quite a glorious time.

Fall is the Time for Mellowing

This morning I am washing citrus storage boxes by the river. As I stoop on a flat rock, my hands feel the chill of the autumn river. The red leaves of the sumacs along the river bank stand out against the clear blue autumn sky. I am struck with wonder by the unexpected splendor of the branches against the sky.
—Masanobu Fukuoka

FOR ME, FALL STARTS with a frenzy of activity. Gotta get the daffodils in the ground! Clean up the spent irises, peonies, cranesbills! Hurry up and repot all the young shrubs and trees into larger containers for their winter rest! As the sun sets sooner each day and hours in the garden shrink, I panic. How will I ever get it all done before frost?

But then, as the first seedless Champagne grapes ripen and the aroma of sweet fruit fills the air, I take a break to enjoy the garden's last offerings. I stop to pick a cluster of these petite, sweet grapes and sit under the arbor to enjoy them. When I go back for just a few more, I notice that the large, cone-shaped panicles of 'Pinky Winky' hydrangea have turned a soft shade of pink. 'Pinky Winky' is one of a half dozen hydrangeas growing on the north side of the arbor where the grape leaves shade them from summer's heat. With a soaker hose to keep them moist and no tree roots to compete with, they're the happiest hydrangeas in the whole garden.

I cut a bunch of dahlias for the house and arrange them in a bouquet. Early in October, all the pink, coral, and dark burgundy dahlias are flowering like crazy, as if to make up for their late start. In summer I'm stingy about cutting flowers—they last so much longer outdoors—but now that the garden is winding down, I take them inside for a closer look.

Many roses are also making a resurgence. 'Lovely Fairy' is not only covered with deep pink flowers, but is packed with buds for yet one more burst of color. The silky pink and orange blossoms on 'Mutabilis' rose are bigger than they were all summer and seem to glow in the autumn light. 'Coral Flower Carpet' rose has never stopped blooming since early summer and looks as good now as it did in June.

True, lots of leaves are declining, especially on many poor faded hostas, but the hardy fuchsias make up for them. 'Zulu King' is a waterfall of wine-colored flowers, long and slender, while my favorite, 'Cricket', flaunts brilliant coral flowers.

Last spring, a friend shared some sweet alyssum that he grew from seed, and I tucked them around the the fuchsias, mostly for the fragrance. The alyssum bloomed once, then I cut it back in late summer, and now it's flowering again, a froth of white lace underpinning the more glamorous fuchsias.

I've complained about self-sowing asters that spring up everywhere in the garden, some in washed-out colors like pale lavender. But I change my mind when drifts of volunteer asters in all shades of pink and purple bloom together with yellow three-leaved coneflower (*Rudbeckia triloba*). On autumn days that start out overcast, followed by a misty rainfall, I love any flower that brightens the garden.

By the middle of October, I realize I'll never get all the fall tasks finished, so I give up and relax into the season. I settle for getting the daffodil bulbs, potted hostas, and ferns planted in the ground by Thanksgiving. I vow to move the young Japanese maples I've been growing into larger pots, very soon—but not today. Other jobs can wait for winter. That's when topping the paths with wood chips will give me a good enough workout to stay warm. That's when I'll prune the dead wood inside the climbing and shrub roses and dig out more Siberian irises.

Fall is for mellowing out—for enjoying the light as long into the late afternoon as it lasts, for looking at the garden with appreciation for all that it has given. Volunteer 'Sungold' tomatoes from last year's plants have been the best ones this year—thank goodness I didn't weed them out by accident. They're so sweet and I graze on so many out in the garden that they never make it into the house. In a pinch, the purple seedpods on *Fuchsia hatschbachii* also make a sweet snack.

Any day now the gorgeous pink, purple, and green clusters of Concord grapes dangling from the arbor will be ripe enough to feast on. One good frost enhances their flavor from good to heavenly. Isn't it amazing that the very same dip in temperature that blackens the dahlias turns the grapes even sweeter?

Autumn Musings

> . . . *this morning I saw light kiss*
> *the silk of the roses*
> *in their second flowering,*
> *my late bloomers*
> *flushed with their brandy.*
> *A curious gladness shook me.*
> —Stanley Kunitz

As the light wanes just a tiny bit each day and the plants slow down, I treasure the garden all the more. I feel less rushed in autumn and more attentive to the small details that make living in my garden so compelling.

I glance out the window to see a squirrel racing up the enormous sweet gum tree with a large meal in its mouth. I grab the binoculars to see what he's found—is it a pear, or a fig, or an apple? No, it's a sunflower that's gone to seed. Stretched out on a broad limb, the squirrel clutches the chunky flower head with both front paws and nibbles on the seeds like he's eating corn on the cob. He's very thorough, turning the circular pod around and around to get every morsel. It's a meal on a wheel! It's autumn, and the garden's bounty is rolling in.

I go outside and snip off a dozen sunflower pods from the tall flowers that are gradually going to seed and place them in the birdfeeder nailed to the sweet gum's trunk. I watch more squirrels find the seedpods and haul them up the trunk to stout tree limbs where they eat their fill. I'm not worried about the birds—there are plenty of seeds on the asters and millions of bugs for them to feast on.

Hundreds of bees gather on the large flat pink discs of

'Matrona' sedum. They're so cooperative, sharing the space as swarms of their kin arrive to feed. Dozens of flowers—plentiful platforms full of color and nourishment—offer up their nectar. The bees go about their business and pay me no attention as I peer into their humming world. No matter how different we creatures are, we all must eat to survive.

Mexican orange, normally a spring bloomer, is flowering again this fall, and hummingbirds flit back and forth between its round, white flowers and summer jasmine's funnel-shaped blooms. Even though books say hummingbirds like red and orange, clearly they're happy enough with white.

The dangling flowers of Himalayan honeysuckle have turned to wine-colored berries that are soft and ripe. Plantsman Maurice Horn once told me they taste like burnt caramel and sure enough, one little bite confirms his description. But what I'd really like is a pair of earrings just like these long chains of tiny lanterns.

Nearby the scent of caramelizing sugar fills the air around the katsura tree. As its leaves turn golden in fall, they emit the tantalizing fragrance of a bakery, but where is my cookie? A little further along the ripening Concord grapes add their aroma to autumn's perfume. I stop to taste one, linger to eat just a few more, and finally cut a long stem of plump purple fruit to take with me as I roam. I make a mental list of friends who might like grapes for making juice or jelly. Autumn's abundance is the perfect excuse to reconnect after a busy summer.

Heading for shade, I decide that deadheading the masterwort is the perfect job on this hot afternoon—not too strenuous and quick to bring satisfying results. Masterwort opens its white lacy flowers all summer and fall, and snipping off the spent flowers not only refreshes the plant's appearance, but prolongs the bloom time.

As I'm peacefully pruning back the long stems filled with tan flowers, I feel a sharp pinch on my finger. I've been stung! Emergency bells go off in my system. Bee stings aren't life-threatening to me, but I've learned from experience that this finger will swell up and itch for days. I run to the garage for a bottle of household lemon ammonia, dip a kleenex in the liquid, then swab my finger. A friend shared this remedy with me, and it helps reduce the inflammation. I go in the house and take a Benadryl for itching. But despite all this, my whole hand puffs up hugely. "It looks like a baby's hand," says my husband, Tom, later that evening. It's true—all the lines and wrinkles have disappeared as the skin has stretched out. Can this be the new Botox?

Even so, the next day I am able to hold a shovel, to dig and plant, to turn compost. I stay away from the bed where I got stung. Early in the morning while it's still cool out, I add fresh attractant to the yellow jacket traps. While I'm at it, I clean out the hummingbird feeder and pour in fresh sugar water.

Nearby, the yellow wax bells catch my eye. They began flowering in August and are still opening, and even though they're subtle, this late in the season any dab of color is welcome. I like this shade-loving perennial for its handsome maple-shaped leaves that contrast nicely with lacy maidenhair fern and delicate sweet woodruff. At its feet the dazzling lavender-pink flowers of autumn crocus put on their fall show. This wonderful but weird bulb sends up leaves without flowers in spring, and flowers without leaves in autumn, so I've placed it amid hellebores whose foliage surrounds the crocus's naked flowers. I bought the original bulb at Beth Chatto's nursery in England way back in 1994, and this year I count thirteen flowers. When they're done blooming, I'll poke around to see if there are enough bulbs to separate and replant. I'd love to spread the color further along the bed.

It seems that overnight the false aster, which was nothing but a tall mass of gray-green foliage, has burst into a bouquet of radiant white daisies, and turtle flower has lit up with bright pink blossoms. Fuchsias are offering their final surge of bloom, especially 'Yolanda Frank', a fountain of peach blossoms. Porcelain berry vine is turning turquoise, and 'Lady in Black' aster is opening its first tiny white stars. The pleasures of autumn are many, with the promise of more yet to come.

Accepting Change

Creative Solutions: One Step at a Time

Then do not grasp at the stars, but do life's plain, common work as it comes, certain that daily duties and daily bread are the sweetest things in life.
—Robert Louis Stevenson

FROM THE BEGINNING my garden was one problem after another. When I first moved in, the whole backyard was a grassy field with a sawdust path running down the middle, just like a freeway. Apple and plum trees dotted the property as if someone had plopped them down helter-skelter, in a big hurry to get them in the ground. On a sunny slope a group of rhododendrons with scorched leaves looked like survivors of a forest fire. Nearby two vase-shaped 'Kwanzan' cherry trees with bubble-gum pink flowers stretched their stiff limbs over a bog.

Most people would have fled from these sad sights, but here's what I saw: a big, mostly flat and sunny space where I could experiment to my heart's content. Coming from a small city lot, the possibility of growing plants on nearly an acre seemed like paradise.

The truth is, I hadn't even begun to grasp the enormity of the difficulties that lay ahead. Heavy clay soil turned soupy in winter and cracked like the Alvord Desert in summer. Pervasive horsetail rush and ground morning glory had made themselves at home on this wetland. Blackberries, ivy, buttercup, and wild mint crept in from the three neighboring properties. But all those problems challenged me to be inventive and stirred up my creative juices like nothing I'd ever experienced before.

Looking back, I have to laugh at my early efforts to tame an acre in one summer. I sprayed herbicide on a huge part of the garden, preparing to plant most of it that first year. Months later, humbled, I settled for developing one long border about halfway down the backyard to screen the lower half from sight. That way I could face the smaller job of planting the area between the back of the house and this long border, one island bed at time, and ignore what was beyond, until later.

"One step at a time" became my mantra. Step one, outline the shape of a bed. Step two, forget about Roundup. Instead, lay down thick layers of newspaper soaked in water to smother the lawn and top it with plenty of mulch and compost. Step three, lay out the plants in their pots and move them around until their pattern makes me happy. Step four, dig the planting holes, sprinkle in some slow-release fertilizer, and plant.

Becoming a gardener has been a long and interesting journey, with an endless education. In some ways it's like learning to conduct an orchestra of plants and inventing ways for them to grow harmoniously together. In time I started thinking of the plants as duets, trios, quartets, and quintets—more like chamber music than symphonies. I began arranging them in smaller and more manageable seasonal vignettes instead of trying to make a huge border all at once—not to mention an entire garden!

I also discovered that a lot like home remodeling, solving one problem in the garden often leads to a host of new ones, so that sometimes it is safer to do nothing. But I'm not very good at doing nothing; actually my downfall is that I'm terrible at doing nothing!

One big eyesore kept bugging me until finally something had to give. A huge, multi-trunked pussy willow, original to the property, loomed menacingly over the fence between my property and my neighbor's, growing taller and wider each year. It was straight out of a horror movie, with craggy limbs that stretched out like gigantic claws. But it also screened the two-story white house next door. Removing it would mean a radical change in the view. Then I noticed that the trunks had grown so thick they were pressing against the fence. It was time to take it down.

In less than three hours the tree service removed all traces but the stumps. Now there was sun, there was light, and there was a two-story white house staring at me. What to do? The space around the willow was a drainage ditch, likely the main reason the prior owners planted it there in the first place, to suck up the water. But I wouldn't be able to plant anything beautiful there to screen the neighboring house. In front of the ditch stood my two enormous compost bins, very useful, but not a pretty sight. Now that I'd saved the fence from danger, how could I transform this newly exposed space?

Each day I stared at the area, trying to imagine how to plant enough tall trees and shrubs to screen a two-story house. But the compost bins were right in the way! Planting anything in front of them would block my access to the bins. The whole situation seemed hopeless, and I regretted taking down the willow, ugly as it had been. "I think I made a huge mistake!" I said to Tom.

"No, you had to take that tree out. You'll find a solution if you keep daydreaming. You always do," he said, in his encouraging way.

Finally, after more restless nights, the light bulb exploded in my brain. I saw that I wasn't finished destroying. I needed to tear out the ugly bins, build a raised bed in their place, and plant it with interesting trees and shrubs for a privacy screen.

It would take time and work, one step at a time. Step one, tear out the bins with a little help from my friends and a sledge hammer. That part was easy and fun, especially when two teenage neighbor boys stepped up to demolish the bins, complete with grunts and shouts. Step two, use the compost within the bins to build a raised bed. Also easy, using a shovel and a rake, as the compost was nice and soft. Step three, find some broken sidewalk, used bricks, and chunks of stone to retain the bed. This took longer, as I posted a request for these materials on a garden society's LISTSERV. I drove around town, picking up these materials from gardeners who were glad to recycle their leftovers. Some folks even helped me load my car! Step four, decide which of the many shrubs and trees already growing in my stash of collected plants would be best for screening.

Now we're talking about the fun part. I selected 'Sekkan Sugi' Japanese incense cedar with golden needles and 'Red Fox' katsura tree with burgundy leaves for height and foliage interest, and alternate-leaved butterfly bush for summer flowers. Thanks goodness for a new project to keep me happy!

The Worried Gardener

The most noteworthy thing about gardeners is that they are always optimistic, always enterprising, and never satisfied. They always look forward to doing better than they have ever done before.
—Vita Sackville-West

THIS YEAR I'VE HAD more than my share of worries in the garden. First there's the passion flower vine that doesn't bloom. Not that it isn't vigorous. Its rambling roots pushed through the container's drainage holes and rooted down in a crack between some patio pavers. New stems scrambled up and over the tops of all my potted plants—now shading them like a gigantic canopy.

I worry that there's not one flower, not even a bud, just foliage, foliage, foliage. Is it a late bloomer? If I wait a little longer will it burst into spectacular bloom? Or is it just a nuisance that will smother the potted camellias trying to grow upright?

I worry about the sex of my wonder trees. Years ago, on a cold winter day at Wave Hill, I saw a gorgeous grove of wonder trees bearing chains of brilliant orange berries. I had to have some for my own garden! I begged for seed and started plants, growing them in pots for years before planting seven young trees in the ground. You need boys and girls to produce fruit, but no one knows exactly how to tell the boys from the girls until they flower.

Naturally, mine haven't bloomed yet. A friend in Seattle with established trees said that males have branches that reach upward at an angle, while females are taller, with layers of horizontally outstretching branches. When I planted mine, I selected several shorter trees with angled branches and some taller ones with layered branches. I squinted a lot to see the shapes of these saplings and hoped for the best. Two years later they still haven't bloomed, and of course there's no fruit yet. Will this be like the passion flower, with nothing but leaves? I worry about this.

Then there are the cracks that appear in the ground every summer, as the clay-based soil dries out and shrinks. Each year this happens, and each year the rains eventually arrive and as the ground swells the cracks fill, but still I worry. It's been hotter and drier this summer than ever before. More cracks have formed at the edges of beds and in the rough lawn at the far end of the garden. I've been filling them with wood chips to help hide them. But will this be the year when the cracks turn to sink holes? One night I dreamt that the backyard had collapsed into a large pond with streams flowing through the beds. I woke up more worried than ever.

Then there's my 'Fuyu' persimmon tree. This year it's formed loads of fruit, but here it is late September, and they're still green. Will there be enough warm sunny days for the fruit to turn orange and become sweet and crisp? Will they ripen before cold weather hits and ruins them?

I fret that I've planted the persimmon too close to a 'Bosc' pear, that it doesn't get enough sun, that it's the wrong variety. Should I plant 'Early Fuyu' that ripens sooner? Not only that, but the pears looks unhappy, with speckled fruit. Maybe fruit trees are too much trouble?

And what about my hardy dwarf banana? Should I plant it in the ground now, in hopes it will live through winter, or stuff it into the greenhouse with all the other tender plants? Will there be room for it along with the countless tender treasures—silver spears with metallic leaves, New Zealand cabbage trees with burgundy blades, succulent echeverias and prickly agaves, not to mention red and peach flowering maples, gifts from friends this summer?

Worried about how much I worry, I turn to *The Gardener's Year* by Karel Capek for consolation. "We gardeners live somehow for the future; if roses are in flower, we think that next year they will flower better," he writes. Maybe all this worry is just my way of making sure that next year the garden will be even more beautiful. And it will be!

Editing My Garden

Have nothing in your house that you do not know to be useful or believe to be beautiful.
—William Morris

LIKE A CLUTTERED CLOSET, my overplanted garden was driving me crazy. Nearly thirty years ago, I couldn't wait for the borders and island beds to fill in. Now the beds were overflowing, actually cramped and crowded with too many plants.

All would be well in paradise if only plants grew at the same rate and multiplied reasonably. Who knew that lady's mantle, which I'd loved for its lobed leaves that collect the morning dew, and sprays of chartreuse flowers that are great in bouquets, would become a thug, seeding down from one end of the garden to the other? Or that lungwort would take over an entire island bed?

In the early years I welcomed all this fruitful multiplying on my acre of wetland. I actually encouraged hellebores to spread by shoveling compost beneath their ripe seedpods, so they germinated right into a rich seed bed. I adored self-sowing annuals like *Verbena bonariensis*, with flowering stalks chock full of tiny purple flowers that passersby stopped to admire. I felt grateful for the Siberian iris, giant maiden grass, cape fuchsia, red twig dogwood, and false spiraea that expanded into hefty clumps.

But as the years flew by, these enthusiastic plants covered so much ground that there was little room left for anything new. Imagine, an entire acre all filled up! When I looked around it hit me—I had way too many of the *same* plants.

Where would I find space for the new epimediums,

dwarf conifers, and hardy fuchsias that I wanted to grow? I could either move to a bigger garden, and work even harder, or come to my senses and edit ruthlessly. I would give away any plants I could pass along in good conscience, and send the rest to the yard debris can.

What could I live without?

I pictured the plants that no longer made me happy and made a list. That was the easy part. Then I heard a little voice whisper, *Who are you to kill perfectly innocent plants?* A huge wave of guilt flooded me and I got stuck.

I pondered the question. *Hmmm.* After some contemplation, the answer popped up like one of those thought balloons hanging over the head of a character in the comics. *I am the boss of my own garden!* Guilt would have to go, right along with the undesirable plants. If I wanted to renew the garden, I'd have to destroy before I could create. I promised myself to stay strong and edit with a firm hand.

That process reminded me of an experience I'd had as a younger gardener. Visiting Great Dixter for the second time, I was shocked to see that Christopher Lloyd had dug up all his roses and planted tropicals in their place. Now, closer to the age he was when he made this radical change, I understood. Gardeners change, and gardens change right along with them.

Out, Out, Out! Raspberries went first. A well-intentioned friend had given me a few starts of 'Fall Gold', and while I wasn't looking, they'd run swiftly throughout a long border, creeping beneath roses and galloping through penstemons and fuchsias. The fruit was tasty, but the prickly canes needed thinning and pruning every year. The "ouch" factor and continual managing put them at the top of my "Out" list. I could buy a few boxes of raspberries at the market and skip all that work. In their place I'd grow newer varieties of peegee hydrangeas and ferns, which would be much easier to care for.

More shrubs that ran relentlessly underground went next—I removed long stretches of red twig dogwood and false spiraea to make room for new varieties of oakleaf hydrangea and andromeda. Weeks of labor followed: digging deeply with mattock and spade and chopping off woody roots with long-handled loppers until every shred of the undesirables was gone.

Perennials that bloomed for short periods were next on my hit list. I gave away masses of Siberian and Japanese irises to younger gardeners. Beautiful as they were, I could enjoy them in other folks' gardens. Now I'd have more room for hummingbird mint and new varieties of salvia that intrigued me.

Next to go were daylilies in colors I didn't like any more—pale orange, murky lavender, fluorescent yellow. Roses repeatedly suffering from black spot and rust became history. I'd treasure the healthy ones that much more, especially 'Lovely Fairy', 'Westerland', 'Mutabilis', and 'Robin Hood'.

Hardest to edit were the trees. To me, the presence of trees with sturdy trunks and gracefully spreading branches makes a garden feel more permanent. The birds that I so enjoy find shelter and build nests within their protective canopies. Yet when blight attacked my purple filbert beyond all help, it was time to take it down. When the mulberry tree grew so tall, wide, and craggy that it looked like it belonged beside a haunted house, I decided to cut it down. There were many more suitable trees I could grow in their places. The same fate met a golden curly willow that grew relentlessly tall despite yearly pruning. Fortunately I found a creative woodworker who salvaged the wood for a project, a saving grace.

Now that the guilt is gone, editing has become a sweet pleasure, a major aspect of gardening with joy. The garden can breathe again and so can I.

Wishing for Something Else

> Be content with what you have, rejoice in the way
> things are. When you realize there is nothing
> lacking, the whole world belongs to you.
>
> —Lao Tse

WHENEVER IT SNOWS, I long for the good old days of just plain rain. In the rain, I can still rake, weed, and cut back old foliage, but snow puts an end to all gardening. Pretty as the fat white flakes are as they float hypnotically in the air, their descent signals a sad separation from my beloved garden.

When she illustrated my book *Married to My Garden*, artist Kaye Synoground captured my longing perfectly at the beginning of the section called "Absence Makes the Heart Grow Fonder." Her drawing shows a woman in a bathrobe sitting in an overstuffed armchair, looking out at the winter garden with a cat curled up at her feet. She leans towards the window as if she'd like to fly out there. That's exactly how I feel when it snows.

So when the rains return I'm grateful to see raindrops again, at least for a while. It's warmer out, the wind has subsided, and there's plenty to do. Hundreds of hellebores need their leaves cut back before the new flowers arise. Thousands of slugs wait for me to send them to their next incarnation.

But then, after a week of rain, I begin wishing for sun. Just a few days of it, or even a few hours each afternoon. The forecast shows nothing ahead but rain. The extended forecast fills me with gloom. The cheerful sun icon is weeks away. I remind myself how often forecasts are inaccurate, but still, wanting, craving, and longing surge through me like tidal waves. I tell myself it could be worse. I could be in Chicago, or Buffalo, or Fairbanks. But it's no use. Like a lot of other times, what do I want? Something else.

Comedian Jerry Seinfeld did a bit about this in one of his standup routines. He said that we love to go out on the town, but before the evening is even over, we long to be back home. We get all dressed up to go out for some fun, then we can't wait to get home and relax in our bathrobes. Neither place is satisfying for very long. And so it is in the garden. When it snows we want rain; when it rains we want sun; when it's sunny for days on end we wish for rain. We seem to be wired to always want something else.

And yet, deep down, underneath all the angst, there's a calm layer of awareness that whispers the truth to me. *Right now is all I have. Just this moment.* As I write, rain pours out of the gray skies and rivulets form in all the low spots in the garden. Snug in my office, I sip peach tea. Kitty Webster lounges nearby on his purple rug beside the window, eyes closed but not quite asleep, his ears perking up at the slightest sound. Rain thrums on the leaves and ticks against the window.

My two wheelbarrows lie idle on the lawn, upside down so they don't fill with rainwater, waiting. After years of metal wheelbarrows that rusted I bought two made of poly, and fitted them both with solid-core tires to avoid blowouts. My long-handled, extra-wide rake leans against the potting shed wall, waiting. Its aluminum shaft and resin head are impervious to rain. My aluminum spade, with a round handle like a green Life Savers candy, also stands waiting like a sentry, marking the place where I left off digging.

Winter is a waiting time. Bulbs sleep underground, waiting for some warmth to signal them to send up their green shoots. Ferns and grasses lay collapsed on the garden floor, taking a break from the energetic business of unfurling and growing.

Yet small signs of returning life are already appearing. Through the living room window I see that purple filbert branches are dotted with small pinkish catkins, hinting of spring's glorious, pleated leaves. The sweet box is budded up and any day now will open scented white flowers. Every so often a flash of hot pink winks at me from the ground—winter-blooming cyclamen have naturalized throughout my garden.

Later, needing to connect with green plants, I'll head for the greenhouse to inhale the damp scent of soil and to admire the baby heucheras and infant sedums, rooting down from cuttings and slips. In winter, I turn off the irrigation pipes to the garden in case of freezing weather. Rainwater collects in buckets outside the greenhouse, and I dip in a ladle to water plants on the benches inside. I think of the abundance of water we have and feel grateful, especially when I remember Precious Ramotswe in *The No. 1 Ladies' Detective Agency*, set in Botswana, and how she treasured every morsel of moisture, saving water carefully for her pumpkins, squash, and melon plants. If the rain is anything short of a deluge, I'll rake some more leaves into mounds, to be carted to the compost pile on a drier day.

I will probably never stop wishing for something else, something better, shinier, newer, more exciting. But when I stop and stay present for whatever is right in front of me, I feel calmer, happier, more satisfied. It's like this. We get rain here in the winter and spring, lots of it. Only our minds complain that it's too much. Only our minds keep yearning for something else. Maybe it's time to change our minds.

Love the Garden You Have

> Have no fear of perfection.
> You'll never reach it.
> —Salvador Dalí

SOMETIMES I THINK that gardeners love to complain. Our gardens are too wet, too dry, too hilly, too sunny, too shady, too small, too big. We have unwanted visitors—gophers and moles, deer and raccoons, aphids and slugs. And nothing ever stays the same! Plants grow too slowly at first, and then they mushroom overnight! One thing is for sure. Gardens are never quite right.

Does this come from reading too many garden books filled with pictures of perfection? Or from visiting quintessential gardens like Sissinghurst where roses climb the ancient brick walls and buff young gardeners tend every border with meticulous attention? It's a lot like expecting romantic love to be straight out of the movie *Moonstruck*. Our fantasies take us way beyond the possibilities of real life.

My yoga teacher, Kathleen, who is not only very limber, but also extraordinarily wise, tried to teach me the benefits of an imperfect life. "We're here to learn from each other," she said. "If it were easy, what would we have to learn?"

It's true. I would never even be practicing yoga if my back hadn't rebelled some thirty years ago. At that time, I didn't know the meaning of moderation, and after digging in heavy clay soil for hours, an electric jolt shot down my spine, forcing me to stop. I made an appointment to see an osteopath with a reputation for healing backs.

A dignified man in a white coat and tailored pants,

he adjusted my back and relieved a lot of the tension. But the doctor got my full attention when he knelt down on the floor and showed me how to practice cat/cow, the first yoga pose I'd ever seen. It was all I could do not to giggle at the sight of this dignified man, down on the floor, imitating a cat and a cow. But he was deadly serious—if I didn't learn yoga, I'd have a chronic problem, and I might have to give up gardening. Terrified at that possibility, I signed up for a beginner's class, and a whole new world of stretching and strengthening opened up.

It's the same in the garden. If it were already perfect, what would we have to learn? Why would we bother to join garden groups where we commiserate and learn from each other? Problems with plants send us looking for friends who can help. I took my first Master Gardener class in 1980 so that I could rub shoulders with more experienced gardeners. That was the beginning of an adventure rich with friendships, gardens, and travel.

The joy, it seems, is in the process. Of course, it was hard to remember that concept when I raked up millions of sweet gum fruit that fell each year from the enormous tree that shaded the south side of my house. It was only when I remembered how welcome that cool shade was in the heat of summer that I would stop whining about the spiny little balls that took hours to haul to the yard debris can. When I thought about how that tree stood stoically through rain and wind, snow and ice, sturdy limbs stretched out to bless the garden, how could I mind doing my small part?

I don't recommend that you rush out to plant a sweet gum—it really belongs in a park. But mine was here to stay until the day that it began to shed enormous limbs and became too dangerous to keep. After I had it taken down, I grieved for weeks and spent many sleepless nights trying to figure out how to renew the garden in its absence. I still miss its cooling shade every summer, and the entertaining acrobatics of squirrels chasing each other up its stout trunk.

I have a wetland garden, and I moan about that, too. A friend recently said that I garden in a swamp, and for a while I felt very inferior. I asked myself, "Should I just move, and be done with all the wet soil?" But when summer's drought arrives, I'm grateful for the moisture-retentive clay that sustains many of the plants through summer's heat. Of course the ground cracks so severely by the end of summer that I could drop a trowel down one of those gullies and never see it again. A visitor once asked, "How do you get those cracks to look so artistic?" I gave her my Mona Lisa smile. A little mystery is always good.

Making the most of gardening on a wetland, I've researched plants for damp places. I grow every kind of willow, red and yellow twig dogwoods, and plenty of tough shrub roses. Anything with "marsh" in the name is happy in my garden, especially marsh marigold and marsh spurge. Siberian, Japanese, and spuria irises have made themselves at home, and the calla lilies are lush, with seedlings showing up as mostly welcome surprises, far from the original clump.

I have made my peace with moles, well almost. I don't want to spend my days trapping them and burying the dead, so I firmly tromp down their hillocks and they continue to tunnel and send up new mounds here and there. It's only soil, and sometimes I even go so far as to call the moles my "little tillers." I only get aggravated when they start churning up the so-called lawn, a green blanket of buttercup and clover with a little grass mixed in. Even then, it's easy to mash down the disturbed earth and before long the green grows back.

With all its flaws, my garden has moments of

perfection when I least expect them, just like love for another person that arises suddenly without any deliberate effort. In a drenching rain, while I'm cutting back hundreds of 'Ogon' sweet flags to freshen their golden blades, I look up to see the tiny bronze leaves of the katsura tree emerging, pairs of adorable little hearts all along each branch. Squishing through the front lawn I notice two epimediums blooming in perfect harmony, one purple and the other orange. And as I get halfway down the backyard, I see a pair of ducks waddling through the wet border in search of slugs. He's got his gorgeous green cap on and she's a more modest brown. A second fellow approaches, and soon both boys are quacking heartily. Who will win the girl?

How lucky to be in the presence of so many wonderful surprises, even if my garden is a wetland on heavy clay where the canvas is never finished. What would I do with my sweet time if it were perfect?

In Praise of Small Pleasures and Ordinary Gardens

*The ordinary acts we practice every day at home
are of more importance to the soul
than their simplicity might suggest.*

—Thomas Moore

LATELY I'VE BEEN WALKING in my neighborhood early in the morning and enjoying the small touches of beauty sprinkled about front yards. A stately palm tree spreads its wings beside a triple-decker bird feeder, where a flock of chickadees enjoy their breakfast. Three fat sunflowers facing the road make me smile. A persimmon tree is loaded down with green fruit, and I hope they will ripen in time for the owners to enjoy them. Maybe they'll even share a few with me.

Many of these delights belong to ordinary gardens where a designer has never set foot. Most likely busy families live here, and time for gardening is scarce. Plants are stuck in the ground here and there without any pattern—a cherry tree, some blueberry bushes, a few rose shrubs dotted around for color, a lone fuchsia basket dangling from a porch ceiling. Pink, orange, and red zinnias bloom happily together. No one here is worrying about color clashes.

I love these signs of everyday gardeners who don't take growing plants too seriously. Buddhism speaks of "beginner's mind," that refreshing state of awareness when everything is new and possible. I remember how gardening was like that for me early on, before it became my career. I loved growing velvety purple petunias and lipstick red geraniums, white sweet alyssum and bright yellow and red marigolds. I want to recapture that feeling of discovery and surprise.

For example, lately, one of my biggest thrills is going down to the former pond in the lower part of my garden. When a landscaper dug out that area, we were certain the heavy clay would naturally hold water in the rainy months. I had visions of ducks and geese and blue herons coming to live in my garden. But each winter the water level sunk lower. The pond was a flop.

At first I filled it with leaves, grass clippings, weeds, and kitchen debris, intending to turn it back into a bed. But wait a minute—here stood a huge composting area generating fertile soil. Now every other autumn I go down to the pile, pull away the topmost layer, and harvest the compost. It's soft and silky, dark as devil's food cake, and perfect for mulch. I run my hands through the mix to remove twigs and any remnants of noxious weeds like morning glory runners. Then I scoop it into buckets that I take to the greenhouse for winter potting and shovel it into wheelbarrows to blanket the beds with mulch. As a child growing up in New York City, I never played in the dirt. Now I'm getting my fill. Sheer bliss.

When I look at the garden with a "beginner's mind" I enjoy the sudden eruption of false aster's white flowers in October, even though they don't pair up with any companions for a stylish vignette. The long stems sway with the breeze, doing an autumn dance, brightening an overcast day with light. Nearby, a few last clusters of deep pink 'Lovely Fairy' roses offer some cheer. Fall means the end of their final bloom cycle, and I love each little flower for this last burst of color. Soon the rose bush will be quietly green, and eventually bare, as nature's cycles keep turning, so I treasure these last blossoms all the more.

Lately I've been dreaming of growing individual plants

in containers and giving up the effort of matching them up with each other in riveting combinations. Yes, there's pleasure in designing, but there's also relief in letting go of striving for perfection. I'm remembering the elderly man who owned my property before I bought it and how he'd plunked down trees and shrubs in the ground any which way, as if he'd dropped them from a helicopter—an apple tree here, a plum tree there, here a juniper, there a grape vine. Originally I was appalled by the chaos, but now I'm wondering if he felt freer and more relaxed in his garden than I do.

Maybe it's time for me to love my garden just the way it is, to cherish each plant and think less about painting a perfect picture. Dwarf conifers have become a new passion, but they don't really fit in with the roses, lilies, and clematis. So what! I plant them in containers and plop them here and there at the front of the beds where I can admire them, especially in winter when my other loves go dormant. It's my garden and I'll plant it my way.

When a bunch of us gardeners were talking about what we would do differently in the next gardening season, I said I wanted to play more and work less. To honor that intention, I've named my garden Barbara's Playground.

Kali Helps Me Garden

The urge to destroy is also a creative urge.
—Pablo Picasso

LATELY I'VE BECOME Kali, the Hindu goddess of destruction. You've probably seen sculptures or drawings of the fierce warrior with her wild hair, furrowed brows, and red tongue. Wearing a necklace of skulls and a skirt of human arms, holding a severed head in one of her four hands, Kali is a terrifying vision. Her ferocious energy combats evil and decay—she destroys in order to recreate. And let me tell you, in the garden, I am Kali.

It takes me a while to work up to embodying her. I like to think of myself as a mild, peaceful gardener. But the day comes when I'm full of frustration about a certain part of the garden that's not what I had hoped for. The dwarf purple willow I'd pictured as a silver hedge has turned into a weeping shrub, spilling all over the bed, while the old roses I treasured for twenty years have grown into huge thorny forests. Who knew that Michaelmas daisies and bloody cranesbills would leap from bed to bed? Plants that had once been my friends have become very annoying bullies, hogging the borders and leaving no empty space for new arrivals.

But it's hard to uproot living plants, to say goodbye to shrubs that were once useful. I have to summon up all my determination, and remind myself that it's my garden and I'm the boss of it. I will be Kali, the righteous goddess who destroys in order to transform. I, too, have four arms—if you count my mattock and my digging fork—and wild windblown hair laced with Michaelmas daisy seeds.

Grabbing my mattock gets me in the mood. It's a tool

that means business, with a strong wooden handle and a two-edged blade. One side is like an ax for chopping into roots; the other is a pick that will pierce the most compacted soil. The pick end is also good for prying up rocks that hide underground. A couple of swings with the mattock and I'm on a roll, getting the ground opened and loosening the dense root systems of unwanted invasive perennials like yellow flag irises. When I come across a root from a tough shrub or tree that's traveling beyond its territory, I use the ax blade to chop it free, then pry it out with the pick. I fling all the debris onto a big tarp.

Swinging a mattock harnesses my destroyer energy. It's so empowering! I put my whole weight into it, muscles working to open that soil and remove the undesirables. Next I rake the loosened soil into a smooth surface. Before long the bed is a blank slate waiting for transformation.

Like a marathon runner at the finish line, I feel a great sense of accomplishment. And yet, now I'm also at the starting line of something new. I have liberated a big chunk of what my gardening buddy Doug calls "prime real estate," a sunny space about eight by ten feet, between a fence and a path. How shall I decide what to plant there?

I step back and look at the big picture. To the left, and closer to the fence, are plants showing brilliant fall color—a Chinese pistachio tree turning orange and a Persian ironwood tree glowing yellow and red. Towards the front are burgundy-leaved shrubs—a 'Summer Wine' ninebark, a Chinese fringe flower bush, and a 'Red Jewel' barberry.

To the right of the empty space is a seven sons tree that blooms white in late summer and warms up in September when the flower petals drop and red sepals remain, brightening the branches. Beneath it stretch drifts of Japanese aster with tiny pale blue flowers that bloom in fall. Why not keep this autumn theme going in the new space?

Fortunately, like every obsessed gardener, I have a stash of plants panting to escape from their pot prisons. A stewartia tree that turns red in fall and a purple-leaved 'Penny Lane' ninebark are bursting out of their containers. Their roots poke out of the drainage holes, longing to get in the ground.

I move them into the empty space and picture how they will relate to each other and to the already established beds to the left and right. The stewartia will be perfect between the Chinese pistachio and the seven sons tree. 'Penny Lane' will be another link in the chain of wine-leaved shrubs. These woody plants will be the bones of the new space, for fall color, and in time I'll add daylilies and daffodils.

Now that Kali has cleared the way, I transform back from goddess of destruction to peaceful gardener and begin to plant the bed.

Go with the Flow

*Everything is so fleeting and impermanent.
It's enough to drive you bat shit crazy.*
—Shane Kuhn

HAVE YOU EVER had a dramatic change in your garden as a result of a neighbor's action? Perhaps the trees next door that once shaded your border are cut down and your hostas and hydrangeas are burning up in the sun. Or your neighbor decides to build an addition, and now a larger house looms closer to your property line, casting shade on your rose garden. If there's anything the garden teaches me over and over, it's that everything is impermanent and I'd better learn to go with the flow. For me, this is a hard lesson—I'd much rather not go with the flow, especially when it's someone else's!

Especially one summer, when my garden seemed so satisfying, with more color than ever from roses, dahlias, and daylilies, and lots of berries setting on the viburnums and idesia trees. I was feeling pretty complacent, completely unaware that a big surprise was on its way, one that would challenge me to redo a significant part of the garden. One morning as I began my daily walk I noticed a big truck, loaded with bright yellow plastic tubing and lots of wood, idling in the middle of the road. The driver pointed to an address on his work order and hollered out the window of his truck. "Know where this is?" he asked.

"You're almost there," I said, pointing toward my neighbor's house. When I got back from my walk I heard the sound of hammering, and lo and behold, a two-story play structure was rising up on the other side of my fence.

The egg-yolk yellow, lipstick red, and royal blue plastic slides and climbers were so flamboyantly bright that my mouth fell open. How would I ever relax in my formerly peaceful garden with this blinding structure glaring at me?

I liked my neighbors and their adorable children, and I loved their front cottage garden filled with roses, hydrangeas, and phlox. But the huge play structure, just beyond my coral 'Westerland' roses and visible from most of the backyard, was horrifying. So after I got over the shock, I began to daydream about how to erase it from my view.

But first, let me share the irony in the whole situation. The previous neighbors had grown an orchard of fruit trees in their backyard. The trees shaded and dried out the soil below them as well as the bed on my side of the fence. After many sad plant funerals, I learned that false spiraea could survive in dry shade. I planted a handful of these ferny shrubs in the challenging border. They thrived and multiplied, running underground to form lusty colonies. At four feet tall, they also camouflaged the old board fence that was on its last legs.

New neighbors moved in, cut down the old fruit trees, and installed a handsome cedar fence. Suddenly, the false spiraeas were in full sun. They were beside themselves with joy, growing even more heartily with the return of bright light, and completely filled in the back of the border. I began to think of other more interesting plants that could benefit from this welcome sunshine, but I didn't have the heart to dig up all those thriving false spiraeas.

The arrival of the play structure changed everything. The false spiraeas would never grow tall enough to hide it. Now that I was desperate for screening, I had a perfect excuse to dig them up and find taller sun-lovers, and soon, I had a plan.

Every day for two weeks I worked with purpose, giving my shovel and mattock a workout. False spiraea roots are woody and range far, so it took determination and sweat to get them out. Step one, cut all of the false spiraea back severely for better access to the roots. Step two, dig around each shrub, making sure to go deep enough to sever all the roots. Step three, lift them out and remove all the soil around the roots to lighten the load on the way to the yard debris can. Step four, go inside for a tall drink of iced tea.

There were eight shrubs, and removing each one was a small triumph. Little by little, I emptied that back of the border of all plant life. All along I daydreamed about what to plant once the weather cooled off. At the end of two weeks I raked the soil smooth and admired the new empty canvas.

I needed tall shrubs that would also grow wide, or perhaps small trees that branch low on the trunk. I looked around my stash of plants already growing in big containers, and found a lilac given to me by a neighbor and an elkhorn cedar I'd bought impulsively at a plant sale. At a nursery I found a jumbo 'Black Lace' elderberry. Over the next few weeks I filled in the spaces between these large shrubs with daylilies, cranesbills, and avens for plenty of summer color.

Of course the day came, ten years later, when a third set of neighbors moved in. The red, yellow, and blue play structure was disassembled, and off it went in a big truck. I was glad to see it go, but by then, it really didn't matter. My trees and shrubs were all grown up, and whatever went in next, I would hardly notice.

It's Hard to Let Go

*The secret of survival is to embrace change,
and to adapt . . . Sometimes you have to use your
failures as stepping-stones to success. You have to
maintain a fine balance between hope and despair.*
—Rohinton Mistry

I JUST READ a sad story in Mirabel Osler's *A Breath from Elsewhere* about an elderly woman who sold her large garden and moved to a new house. Two weeks later, she died. I pictured the wrenching shock of leaving a garden and vowed never to leave my own beloved acre.

Yet Osler's warning words about the need to change in older age hit me hard: "Whether you move or whether you remain where you are, unless you adapt and make things easier, more practical and less of a drudgery for yourself, you won't avoid ending by hating the garden. . . . Instead of it being a garden of pleasure, you end up as its prisoner."

In my seventies, I still wield the loppers with plenty of zest. Daily stretches, walking, and regular gardening all help. But two hours of steady gardening is about my limit now. To be honest, I want to spend more time looking and less time whacking. I want more time to putter and fewer beds to mulch. I long for time to sit and read a novel, to write, to see friends. So lately I've been daydreaming about ways to make the garden smaller.

The trouble is, I can't figure out where to draw the line. I love all my plants and I want to keep growing them—to see purple iris open each spring, watch hostas unfurl their puckered blue leaves, witness little grape leaves expand and clusters of fruit dangle from the arbor every summer.

I'd hoped that someday the plants would mature and take care of themselves. I can hear you laughing! Like pets, plants need endless tending. Taking care of the garden, connecting intimately with plants—their branching structure and flowers, their waxing and waning with the seasons—is partly a joy. But I, too, am waning with the seasons of my life, and growing tired.

I was thumbing through a December 1992 issue of *Fine Gardening* the other day. Inside was "Beds and Borders," my first published feature, illustrated by a watercolor rendering of my garden. At the back of the property sits a space marked "Undeveloped Area." Since then, I've planted two mixed borders there. Perhaps it's time to return them to nature, but they're the best borders in the garden!

"Just put a fence in, halfway up the garden," a friend once suggested. What? A fence in the middle would blot out half the beauty, obscuring the giant maiden grass waving in the breeze, erasing the nuthatches flitting through the apple trees. More recently I asked another friend to look at the garden with fresh eyes. She wondered if I could stop pruning down the giant maiden grass and let the old canes decay while new ones came up. Or could I let the lawn behind the grasses turn into a meadow? I tried to picture the change. I saw a huge mess.

I'm not ready for this! It's like dominoes. Let one part of the garden go, and little by little chaos will creep into the cultivated parts, until eventually it will all revert to nature. I guess that's the hard part: knowing that the natural state of a garden is wilderness. When I first came to the garden it was a sunny meadow with tall grasses, dock, and thistle. Occasionally a small snake slithered through, or a frog popped up.

After decades of beating back blackberries and ivy, I'm not ready to give in. Stubborn determination defies good sense. A true Capricorn, earth sign to the core, I dig in my heels instead of embracing change.

Even so, I've reluctantly made a few small changes to nibble away at some of the garden's edges. Two paths toward the back of the garden are easy to close off for a while with some old fireplace screens, allowing me to neglect a small part of the garden.

Is there a new way to look at the wild grasses and buttercups that creep between the perennials in the more remote borders? Can I let them blend in instead of rushing to dig them out? I don't fight them in the so-called lawn. Maybe it's time to make peace with them in a few other places.

I don't regret the passionate path I've taken. How can I possibly put the brakes on when spring fever impels me forward again each year? Just please, Goddess Flora, show me how to live with the weeds while I listen to the songs of the chickadees.

From Despair to Hope When a Giant Tree Crashes

Life and death in the garden are no different than life and death outside the garden. Our options are to dwell on the sadness of death or celebrate the life that passed and embrace the next life that lies ahead.

—Tony Avent

AT THE TOP of my hundred-foot-tall sweet gum tree, a man in a yellow hardhat fired up his chain saw. I let out a deep sigh and watched him take down the only shade tree in my backyard. The saw screamed as it bit into branches, and slabs of wood thundered to the ground below. Three helpers cut the sections into manageable pieces. By the end of the day, only the trunk remained, like a gigantic telephone pole, while wood rounds lay in piles all over the battered lawn.

It had all begun two weeks earlier when I'd been sitting peacefully in the shade of the sweet gum with my neighbor Doug after he'd helped me prune a willow. We heard what sounded like thunder crackling, but it was a sunny September afternoon, with white clouds drifting in a blue sky. Seconds later, a huge limb dropped out of the tree and crashed to the bed below.

"Oh my God!" I yelled. "If we'd been sitting a few feet closer we could have been killed!" I began laughing hysterically from the shock, and so did Doug. He recovered first, then offered to help.

"Let me cut up that branch with my chain saw," he said.

"No, you've done enough today. I'll take care of it tomorrow."

"I like to help," he insisted. "Get used to it." So Doug cut up the limb into logs and stacked them into a tidy pile while I lopped off the thinner branches and hauled them to the yard debris can.

I felt sad that the limb had demolished a favorite ceramic pot, but mostly I was grateful no one was hurt. This had been the driest summer in Oregon history, and the tree was likely stressed. Soon autumn rains would come and all would be well.

But only days later I heard another ominous crack, and down came another limb. My heart pounded as I approached the tree. Trapped beneath the massive branch, a terra-cotta birdbath lay smashed into pieces.

That night my mind struggled to find a solution. I could have the tree pruned to lighten the load of branches. But what if that wasn't enough? More limbs could snap off and someone could get hurt. But if I had the tree removed, there'd be no more shade in the backyard. Where would we sit in the summer heat? The hydrangeas and hostas would scorch, and I would swelter in the south-facing office.

"I'm so confused," I told Doug. "I hate to take down the tree, but right now, I'm scared every time I walk near it. I'm terrified in my own garden!"

"There's your answer," Doug said. "Of all places in the world, you should feel safe in your garden."

Only two days later, I heard a loud snap and looked out the window. A third limb slammed to the ground. It was time. With a heavy heart, I called my tree service. "My poor sweet gum is falling apart—it's already dropped three limbs. How soon can you take it down?"

"I'll juggle the schedule and get a crew out there

tomorrow," the arborist promised. A wave of relief mixed with sorrow washed over me.

In ninety-degree weather, four men labored for several days to cut down the old tree, haul away the wood, and grind out the stump. Afterwards the garden looked forlorn. Confused squirrels scurried across the lawn, looking for their tree. The sun blazed relentlessly on the garden and blasted the south-facing windows.

For days I moped around, shoulders slumped with despair. I talked about the tree to anyone who would listen. At our community library, one of the volunteers gave me a big hug, and said exactly the right thing.

"It's like a death in the family."

"Yes! You really understand," I said. That night tears came for the first time.

Beyond comforting friends, the plants themselves helped me heal. One morning, I noticed viburnum leaves and fern fronds had turned brown from the heat, and I panicked. In a frenzy, I dug up the most vulnerable plants and transplanted them to shadier places. Later on, when I could think straight, I replaced them with roses and daylilies.

As I mulched the soil around the roses, it hit me: there was a silver lining to this situation! Now I had an opportunity to grow more perennials that loved full sun. I could design a brand-new bed to take advantage of the light, using sages and sedums, penstemons and red-hot pokers, dahlias and lilies. Two island beds already punctuated the lawn, and this new one would add even more color.

Scouring the nurseries for heat-loving plants took my mind off the loss of the sweet gum. As I turned my attention toward a new beginning, my creative energy bubbled up and blew away the clouds of despair. The new island bed would be home to fiery flowers—red, yellow, and orange pokers, hot pink penstemons, and burgundy daylilies, with blue sages and agapanthus for contrast. This bold, exciting space would rejuvenate the garden. Imagining all those bright colors dancing together warmed my heart.

I assembled my flamboyant plants on a table out in the garden and shuffled them around, experimenting with different combinations. Then, using a long hose, I shaped an oval in the lawn, filled the area inside with wet newspapers and cardboard to smother the grass, and topped it all with generous loads of planting soil.

While the soil settled, my mind spun with possibilities for creating shade to cool the windows and shelter a sitting space. I could plant a new tree, but what kind, and how long would it take to cast shade? I could design a pergola with vines over the top to create shade more quickly, with a paved area underneath for comfortable seating. Perhaps awnings could shade the south facing windows. Ideas popped up like jack-in-the-boxes—too many at once.

One step at a time, I told myself, trying to calm down my hectic thoughts. I made a list. Visit the awning shop. Stroll through the arboretum to look at trees. Find books on pergola designs. Look at paving materials for a patio.

Weeks went by as a new backyard took shape in my mind. Little by little I made decisions. Retractable awnings cost the earth, but inexpensive, roll-up bamboo shades would work well for now. After looking at trees in nurseries and gardens, I decided on a 'Village Green' Japanese zelkova. While the tree grew big enough to cast shade, I would build an arbor with overhead vines for immediate seating and pave a patio beneath it.

When November arrived, I still missed the towering sweet gum but no longer felt defeated. Looking out my office window, I watched the newly planted zelkova tree drop its autumn leaves and spread its young branches. The perennials in the island bed were settling in, sending down their roots and preparing for a dazzling display next summer. In my heart I knew that my backyard would soon be beautiful again, in a new way.

Transformation

*You have to find something . . . that anchors you,
something that keeps you looking forward, even on the
bad days, when you're tempted to look back.*
—Lisa Gardner

"You must still be in shock," John Stone said.

I'd just told him about losing my giant sweet gum tree at the end of August. I took a deep breath, relieved that this landscape contractor, the fourth one I'd consulted with, really understood what I was going through. The seventy-year-old tree that had reached the end of its life just weeks before had provided shade and a cool sitting space for friends and visitors. An ample patio with a pergola on one end would hopefully serve a similar purpose. That October afternoon, when he took in the garden's long vista with its colorful island beds and acknowledged what an insatiable plant nerd I am, I knew John Stone was my man.

I used to think that hardscaping meant paving a concrete sidewalk in the garden. But I learned through this experience that it can be an expression of a gardener's heart as much as the plants themselves, especially if you work with someone who *gets* you—who understands what you love and is able to translate your thoughts and desires into stone, pavers, concrete, or wood.

Best of all, John dreamt up possibilities I hadn't considered, like pulling the patio away from the house so we wouldn't be sitting in a heat pocket. He suggested leaving plenty of space for perennials and shrubs between the house walls and the hardscape to cool things down and enhance the picture. Not only was he building me a patio, he was giving me room to grow more plants!

The whole process of collaboration was new to me. John allowed plenty of time for us to figure out the shape of the patio and the surrounding beds. First he drafted two possible designs on paper and encouraged me to think about it. He understood how much I like curves, so one of his designs showed a patio shaped like a kidney bean. I wanted it more oval and laid out a hose that was too darn stiff in winter to curve the way I wanted, but he got it. On his next visit, he spray-painted an outline on the ground with chalk and erased it repeatedly with his foot, respraying it until it was just the way I'd imagined.

Next we discussed materials. Would we use exposed aggregate, concrete pavers, or stone?

"I'll measure the square footage, then send you a bid for all three materials, and you can decide on the budget," he said. In his opinion, since the space wasn't that big, the extra cost of stone over the other materials would be minor compared to the extra benefit of stone's beauty in the garden, but it was entirely up to me.

My husband, Tom, and I had already admired varieties of pavers and exposed aggregate in other gardens, but when we visited Smith Rock Inc. a new world opened up. Of the dozens of sample rock slabs standing in bins, the final contest was between bluestone and eagle rock. As the sun glanced off the eagle rock, illuminating its lavender and orange tints, my heart beat faster. Yes! In this once-in-a-lifetime project, eagle rock was the winner. I began dreaming of orange-tinted grasses and purple-flowering perennials to echo the stone's colors.

Still, each pallet of stone was unique, some predominantly orange, others more gray or lavender. I asked John if I could return to the rock yard with him to make our final selection, and we met there on a cold, sunny morning in early January. Our footsteps crunched over the frozen earth as we trekked out to the storage bins in the vast stone yard. He showed me which rock was best for a patio floor—thick enough yet smooth enough on the surface—and we taped off two pallets with the most lavender and some orange in the mix. I left feeling more excited than ever.

Work began two weeks later when a crew of three arrived at 8 a.m. on the dot together with their foreman and John. For the next two weeks, you could set your watch by their early morning arrival, no matter how cold or wet the weather. First came the tear out. Using a sod cutter and a small tractor equipped with a bucket and a fork, the crew removed a mountain of turf, an old lilac, and remnants of sweet gum roots. They also tore out a wooden staircase in preparation for building a new one out of pavers capped with eagle rock. The garden was a noisy construction zone, and it took faith to imagine that this mess would evolve into something beautiful. Some nights I wondered if I'd made a big mistake.

The three men graded the remaining soil with shovels to form a flat surface for the patio, cutting and filling until the levels were just right, then creating a smooth transition from the patio to the lawn with a gently sloping planting bed. They checked and rechecked the grades with a laser level that stood at one end of the garden like a tripod.

Next they brought in gravel for the base of the patio, smoothing and firming it down. Looking at the gravel base at the end of that afternoon, I began to picture the patio we would sit on in summer. But the real excitement began when a truck delivered the tall rock slabs, still standing in their bins. The men carefully unloaded the rock onto the tractor, then drove it into the garden. For days they cut stone and fit the pieces together like a giant jigsaw puzzle, making sure everything was perfectly level, then they swept finer black gravel into the crevices between the stones. The beautiful eagle rock patio stood completed just two weeks from inception.

I never would have guessed how losing a big tree would transform the garden for the best. When a friend turned the bend to the backyard and shouted "Wow! Wow! Wow! This gives a whole new dimension to your backyard!" my heart leapt with joy.

Acknowledgments

WHEN YOU READ this book you'll hear my voice, yet writing a book is not a solo act. In the wings stand mentors and friends who encouraged, supported, and helped me bring what was once the seed of an idea to fruition.

From the beginning, my husband and best friend, Tom Robinson, read each of these stories with careful attention and a red pen. I knew I was cookin' when he laughed or cried. When the writing was dry, he would remind me, "Write from your heart," and I would start over. Since Tom is not a gardener, his eyes would glaze over when there were too many botanical names, and I knew it was time to cut some of the Latin.

Some of these stories first appeared during my seven-year stint as a columnist for the *Portland Tribune* and in garden magazines, journals, and quarterlies. Tom clipped every single one and saved them in a huge stack. When it came time to cull some for this book, we reread them, graded them, and selected the best ones for *Love Letters*. I added more stories over time.

I am grateful to three more readers who carefully combed through the manuscript for errors in grammar, spelling, and punctuation. Author and writing coach Nancy Woods gets a gold medal for taking time away from her own writing to edit my work. My sister, Sarita Nemerow Eisenstark, generously read and edited the manuscript in record time, and returned it with encouraging comments in the margins. Gardening friend and volunteer extraordinaire Carolyn Guinther hunted for any horticultural errors.

Writing is a great pleasure for me, but sometimes I get sidetracked by self-doubts and life's many distractions. Fortunately, loving friends encouraged me to continue and push through to publication. Thank you, dear friends, for your faith in me, especially Doug Barragar, Diane Golner, La Verne Kludsikofsky, Nancy Lamb, and Connie O'Reilly.

I am thankful to illustrator Linda Engstrom, whose delightful sketches and watercolors add beauty and vitality to this book. She embraced the project with contagious enthusiasm, renewing my determination to get the book in print.

My heartfelt gratitude to Tom Sumner and Brenda Jones of Booktown Production for turning the manuscript into a completed book that you can hold in your own hands. Their help was simply the most skillful that I've ever had in all my years of writing.

If you need more information about the botanical names of plants mentioned in this book, I welcome your questions. You can contact me at barbarablossom@hevanet.com for a timely reply.

www.ingramcontent.com/pod-product-compliance
Lightning Source LLC
Chambersburg PA
CBHW071214090426
42736CB00014B/2822